Get Streaming!

Get Streaming!

Quick Steps to Delivering
Audio and Video Online

Joe Follansbee

ELSEVIER

AMSTERDAM • BOSTON • HEIDELBERG • LONDON
NEW YORK • OXFORD • PARIS • SAN DIEGO
SAN FRANCISCO • SINGAPORE • SYDNEY • TOKYO

Focal Press is an imprint of Elsevier

Focal
Press

Focal Press is an imprint of Elsevier
200 Wheeler Road, Burlington, MA 01803, USA
Linacre House, Jordan Hill, Oxford OX2 8DP, UK

Recognizing the importance of preserving what has been written, Elsevier prints its books on acid-free paper whenever possible.

Library of Congress Cataloging-in-Publication Data
Application submitted.

British Library Cataloguing-in-Publication Data
A catalogue record for this book is available from the British Library.

ISBN: 0-240-80559-3

For information on all Focal Press publications
visit our website at www.focalpress.com

04 05 06 07 08 10 9 8 7 6 5 4 3 2 1

Printed in the United States of America

Contents

Foreword

Who would have imagined that a person could sit in front of a computer and listen to radio stations from anywhere around the world, watch the latest video news, listen and watch the hottest new music videos, or even pick from thousands of movies with the simple click of a mouse?

I first experienced the magic of streaming media in 1995 when I listened to my favorite baseball game that was not broadcast on the radio or TV, but on my personal computer. I was in awe. Once my initial sense of amazement had passed, I started to get seriously interested in how much better the experience could be . . . and how much better it *needed to be* to really change the way the world communicates and is entertained.

For all the early excitement about streaming, the fact remained that the end-user experience was woefully inadequate. "Tin can" sounding audio and postage stamp-sized video were exciting indeed for the technology hobbyist in those days, but a pretty poor match for the expectations of the general population. After all, TVs and home stereo systems had already set a quality bar for consumers that streaming, back then, couldn't reach. And then there was "buffering." The 10 seconds that preceded the beginning of playing back the audio or video, which often also happened mid-clip, was in more ways than one a "show stopper." At least, it was for me!

The good news is that technology doesn't stand still. In the case of streaming media, the advancements in technology have been dramatic indeed. In just a few short years, technology has become available that can now deliver a "TV-like" experience for streaming on the Web—at least if you're on broadband. High-quality, full-screen video and CD quality sound and, in fact, better than CD with full surround-sound audio, are possible for today's DSL and cable modem users, and business users can enjoy the same fidelity on their desktop at work. At the same time, the war on buffering is being fought—to great effect. Technology in modern servers and media players can now intelligently work within the constraints of the available network bandwidth to vastly reduce buffering time and mid-stream interruptions. For dialup users, the experience is less dramatic, but nevertheless is worlds better than just a year or two ago.

In my mind, the technology of streaming has crossed a key quality threshold to where it's no longer just a sideshow (or a slideshow!). Streaming media is now an invaluable tool that helps companies communicate more effectively with their tens of thousands of employees—and with their customers. It helps online retailers sell more products by delivering a better and richer retail experience. It helps millions of people around the world stay in touch with their roots and their areas of interests through thousands of online radio stations. It is a vital component of many emerging music and video services, delivering content on demand to media-hungry consumers around the world. And it's helping businesses of all sizes be more productive and informed.

In short, the early excitement about streaming media is now being followed by a realization of how transformative this technology can be. Those already streaming want to do more, and many of those not delivering streaming content are looking to start. The business benefits are too significant to overlook. And hey, it's fun besides!

When Joe contacted me about his book, I was excited to see his focus on delivering practical information to help people get started with streaming media. If you are just now considering streaming, be encouraged—the advancements in technology that have taken place have not come at the expense of usability. Quite the reverse, in fact. As this book will show, modern streaming technology is both powerful and approachable. You can get started easily and grow incrementally as you learn more—including the always-important feedback from your audience.

I hope your experiences as you begin your journey with streaming media only encourage you to do more and more with the technology and realize its full potential. And I hope you find this book provides a great foundation for you to get started on that journey. I think you'll find that it does.

Dave Fester, General Manager,
Windows Digital Media Division
Microsoft Corporation

Preface

I was a writer and producer at RealNetworks in late 1996. The company was called Progressive Networks at the time, and we were on the leading edge of the Internet boom. I read a news story one day about a small radio station in Belgrade, Yugoslavia. The station was recording its news broadcasts in English and putting them on the Internet, using Progressive Networks' RealAudio technology, which had been out for about 18 months.

Students were rebelling in Belgrade against the government of Slobodan Milosevic, the authoritarian president of Yugoslavia. Milosevic had shut down the radio station, called B92. But his police didn't understand that the news about the students was getting out via the Internet. Progressive Networks decided to help B92 by putting some of the station's newscasts on the company's own Internet servers.

I had to call the man who managed B92's Internet connection, Drazen Pantic. It was very late at night in Belgrade. The telephone line from Seattle to Belgrade was scratchy and hollow and Drazen wanted to keep the conversation short. His English was good, but he seemed nervous. We discussed some of the technical details of the project and then I hung up.

I felt afraid for him. I wondered if police were watching him, looking for an excuse to arrest him. I put myself in his shoes, and I wondered whether I could ever defy a threatening force, as he was doing. And here I was, helping him with a new tool called "streaming media" that allowed him and his companions to speak to the world about their wish for freedom. The responsibility weighed on me as if it were one of my young daughters riding on my shoulders. I was happy to bear it.

You are about to discover one of the most fascinating and exciting tools for communication across the Internet and within private computer networks. It has helped home users, small businesses, and mega-corporations speak freely about their hopes and wishes for themselves, their families, and their communities. I would ask you to think carefully about how you use these tools. If you find yourself with an opportunity to lift someone up with them, do it.

Joe Follansbee

Introduction

Purpose of the Book

Get Streaming: Quick Steps to Delivering Your Audio and Video Online introduces you to the technology of "streaming," the process of sending audio and video over computer networks in real time. You will learn all you need to know to put music from your garage band, a recording of your child's first words, and video of your CEO's annual pep talk on the Internet or your internal corporate network. The book will teach you the basics of capturing sounds and moving images to a computer hard drive, converting them to files optimized for Internet transmission, and broadcasting them to whoever wants to listen or watch. We'll also talk about the business of streaming media and some of the opportunities presented by the medium. Above all, our goal is to get you excited about using this groundbreaking technology to broaden the impact of your communications, whether it's to thousands of employees in a large corporation or your extended family.

Scope of the Book

Streaming media covers a broad range of options, software vendors, and networking technologies. This book will focus on the proprietary methods of four major manufacturers that dominate 98 percent or more of the market. The leading vendors, followed by their major streaming brands, are

- RealNetworks (RealPlayer/Helix)
- Microsoft (Windows Media Services)
- Apple Computer (QuickTime)
- Macromedia (Flash MX)

The book will also detail some of the leading non-proprietary streaming technologies, notably the Motion Picture Experts Group (MPEG) set of standards, including MPEG Layer III (MP3) and MPEG-4.

We won't be discussing networking technologies in minute detail or application development, such as writing plug-ins to streaming media servers. We'll also avoid specific computer hardware options, such as hardware audio or video encoders, although we will offer suggestions for building streaming media workstations.

Who Should Read This Book

You should read this book if you work with audio or video in any form, especially if you plan to deliver it over the Internet or a private computer network. Even if you work in a support role or as a decision maker and don't get dirt under your fingernails, as they say, this book will help you understand an important new distribution channel for media properties. Some specific media professionals who will benefit include the following:

- Web designers
- Web programmers
- Videographers
- Audio engineers
- Media producers
- Post-production managers (audio and video)
- Educators
  - Communications and journalism
  - Distance learning
  - Computer science
- Business leaders interested in online media opportunities

Home audio and video hobbyists familiar with computers can also use the information in this book immediately to distribute their projects over the Internet to family and friends.

Whether you are a pro or a tech-savvy home computer user, we wrote this book with some basic assumptions about your computer and Internet knowledge. We assume that you have a

- Minimum one year of experience with a personal computer
- Familiarity with basic Internet tools, e.g., web browsers and FTP programs
- Familiarity with basic computer terminology, e.g., CPU, RAM, and hard drive

By the end of this book, you'll have the basic knowledge to create streaming media all by yourself. However, we suggest you work closely with friends and colleagues as a team, especially when it comes time to broadcast your material over the Internet. Your experience of streaming media will go more smoothly and be more satisfying if you work collaboratively.

Why Learning About Streaming Media Is Important

The Internet pervades our lives. We send pictures of our children via e-mail. We monitor the unfolding of world events on web sites. And increasingly, we listen to music and watch TV-style programming with streaming audio and video. The Internet and its streaming media component have evolved into a mass medium as important as print, radio, and television.

Arbitron/Edison Media Research, a marketing research firm, has tracked the growth of the Internet as a mass medium for audio and video with twice-yearly reports since 1998. Arbitron declared that the Internet had entered the mainstream of American life in its report released in the fall of 2003. Eighty percent of Americans now have access to the Internet from home, work, or a public place, such as a library. Three-quarters of U.S. homes have at least one personal computer, and nearly a third of households have more than one computer. Americans now spend more than an hour a day on average on the Internet.

Arbitron tracks the growth of streaming media in particular. In its fall 2003 report, *Internet and Multimedia 11: New Media Enters the Mainstream*, Arbitron said 50 million people had listened to or viewed streaming audio and video in the past month, and 30 million Americans had listened to audio or watched video streams in the past week.

The growth of the streaming audience matches the growth of broadband Internet connections to the home. A high-quality audio or video experience depends on cable and digital subscriber line (DSL) bandwidth, and once people hook up, they start using streaming media. Arbitron says the number of Americans with broadband at home has tripled since 2001, from 7 percent to 21 percent. One out of six Americans plans to convert from dialup access to broadband, and once they have broadband, they almost double their time online, from 1 hour 16 minutes to 2 hours. And streaming isn't just an American phenomenon. A report from the University of Ferrara, Italy, predicts video streaming traffic in Europe will nearly quadruple between 2003 and 2006.

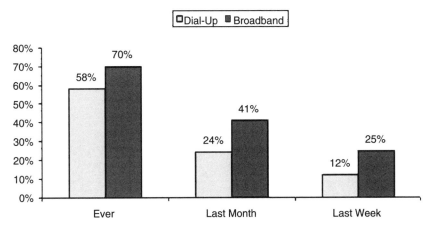

Figure 1 People with broadband connections at home are far more likely to have tried streaming media on a regular basis than people with dialup connections. (Source: Arbitron/Edison Media Research, 2003)

Furthermore, people are starting to get over their initial confusion about streaming technology. The Cable and Telecommunications Association for Marketing said in a 2002 report that 64 percent of Americans know how to listen to music on the Internet, including how to start and stop a stream. Sixty-one percent know how to listen to a live radio broadcast over the Net. They're most interested in music, movie clips, and news clips.

The "Streamie"

Marketers have invented a term for the person who uses online audio or video. The "streamies" have important demographic characteristics that make them attractive marketing targets. The sheer volume of streamies is important to mass-market businesses. More men than women click on streaming media links, and 43 percent of streaming users are between the ages of 25 and 45, a prime age for spending. We'll spend more time on streamies in Chapter 5.

Streaming Media Defined

Streaming media most often refers to the transfer of audio and video data, thought it can be applied to almost any other kind of data, such as static images and text. The data changes in an orderly, logical fashion. Streaming usually includes the interpretation of that data in real time by some sort of software application, usually a "player," such as Windows Media Player.

Most of this book discusses streaming in the context of audio and video. Outside this book, you'll see the word "stream" used for other types of data, such as stock quotes, which we don't cover. Streaming is also frequently confused with downloading files to a computer hard drive. That's just saving a file stored on one hard drive to another. If it's a media file, such as a piece of music, you can't play it until the download is finished. Having said that, there is a streaming term, "progressive download," which is bound to confuse. We'll explain these things throughout the book.

The Streaming Process

Most streaming media systems operate on the client/server model. A client requests data from a server on a computer network, and the server delivers the data, which is interpreted by the client. In streaming media, audio and video data are encoded in a special format that shrinks the data to a manageable size. After the server delivers the data, the client renders the data and displays it as audio or visual information we can understand. We'll take you through this process step-by-step.

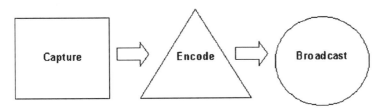

Figure 2   The basic streaming media process. You capture media, encode it to a streaming format, and broadcast it via a streaming server.

Most of the tools for viewing, creating, and in some cases delivering streaming media are available for free or very low cost. It's one of the great things about streaming. We'll walk you through the installation process and show you how to use the basic functions of each tool. We won't show you how to install and configure a streaming media server, however. That requires some administrative and networking expertise that's beyond the scope of this book. But we will give you a good grounding in streaming server technology and terminology, so that you can talk about it intelligently to the powers that be.

The Streaming Media Landscape

Technology doesn't exist in a vacuum. We think it's important to understand streaming media in the context of the overall technical and business environment of the Internet. We've already discussed the broader environment, that is, the fact that the Internet is now deeply entrenched in our lives and that streaming is starting to catch on as a way to enjoy audio and video. Now let's review the technical and business environment of the streaming industry itself.

The Industry

The streaming media industry is one of the most competitive in the Internet software business. The stakes are enormous. Everyone enjoys some form of audio and video, and streaming software manufacturers ultimately want to "own" the method by which you use it on the Internet. They fight for every percentage point of market share, and one of the ways they do it is by one-upmanship in technology.

Progressive Networks (now called "RealNetworks") released the first commercially successfully streaming media technology in 1995. The software was called "RealAudio 1.0." It included a server, an encoder, and a desktop client. The following year, Microsoft released its answer to RealAudio, "Netshow," which was later renamed "Windows Media Services." Thus began a duel between RealNetworks, founded by ex-Microsoft Vice President Rob Glaser, and his old bosses at Microsoft.

Apple Computer entered the competition late with its QuickTime Streaming system in 1998. Despite the loyalty of Apple's user base among media professionals, QuickTime has never caught on as a streaming solution, although it remains important in the arena of digital media production. Sensing this, Apple has sought alliances with RealNetworks as a way to stave off the juggernaut of Microsoft.

The latest major entrant in the streaming media melee is Macromedia, one of the leading companies producing content-creation tools for web designers. Flash MX, the latest version of its Flash animation technology, includes streaming media features. They aren't as sophisticated as the other three vendors, but Macromedia's deep penetration into the web design and production industry suggests it could carve out a significant niche.

Lurking in the wings are several smaller streaming media manufacturers, proponents of open streaming standards such as MPEG-4, media companies, and governments. Lawyers from every side are still hacking away at the Gordian knot of rights ownership in the digital age. The legal problems of Microsoft spice up the stew. Although the antitrust attorneys at the U.S. Department of Justice appear to have backed off their pursuit of the company, regulators in Europe are moving at a determined clip. And don't forget the public relations people at each company. They put enough spin on their products to make planet Earth reverse its rotation. Streaming producers should keep an eye on all these factors, any one of which could affect your streaming plans over the long term.

Your Place in the Landscape

Competition and debate may be good for innovation, wealth creation, and the American way, but it causes migraines for streaming media producers. We all wish computer technology, including streaming media, functioned like other media technologies, such as radio and television—just turn it on and it works. But as long as certain technology companies feel a need to dominate the streaming technological arena, and as long as no single company achieves domination, and as long as people disagree on the right approach to streaming, producers will have to take into account all the possible combinations and variations of each implementation when they offer streams to users. A radio producer doesn't have to worry about whether a listener's car radio can receive his station's signal. A streaming media producer, on the other hand, has to think about the user's computer, bandwidth, installed software, and a universe of other things. This book will help you make the right decisions.

Career Opportunities

Streaming media may excite you enough that you'll want to make it a career. The streaming media industry is still very new, but the streaming media specialist may soon emerge as a true career choice. Media production companies, web hosting firms, and large corporations with internal communications departments will all need people with streaming expertise in the next 3 to 5 years. Jobs could appear in the form of regular full-time employment or as a contracted gig. You will most likely find yourself working in one of three departments, depending on the organization: media production, information technology, or corporate communications. Your best bet today is the IT department. But the pattern of job growth will likely follow the early days of the Internet. Web designers started popping up first in the IT department. Later, they transferred to other departments dealing with media and communications.

Why Use Streaming Media

In the days of the Internet boom, all you had to say was, "It's cool!" for everyone to try a new technology. Those days are gone, thank goodness. Today, the question is, "So what?" Decision makers, especially those holding the purse strings, want to know whether a technology will move an organization toward its goals. Streaming media offers a number of benefits beyond the delight of seeing it work:

Cost-effective method of communication—Organizations save money by reducing certain costs of media distribution. For example, you'd spend about $10 to duplicate and send out a VHS cassette of a training video to a branch office. If you work in a company with operations scattered over a wide geographic area, that cost could run into hundreds or thousands of dollars per video production. If you put that video on a streaming media server, and invite employees to view it online, virtually all the duplication and distribution costs disappear.

Faster time to market—Distribution of audio and video on physical media, such as CD, carries another cost: time. It takes days, weeks, or even months to distribute a video on VHS cassette, for example. However, once the audio or video is produced, you can place it on your streaming server within minutes or hours of its completion. You put a link to it on your web site, announce it to your audience, and they come to you.

Create more options for communications—Today's media environment is more fragmented than ever. People get information from newspapers, magazines, radio stations, televisions networks, web sites, PDAs, even cell phones. Streaming media responds to the audience's desire for a variety of media channels. Adding streaming media as a communication channel gives you a better chance to reach your audience.

Tracking and profiling—When you click on a streaming media link, information about that click is stored in the streaming media server's log. Sophisticated streaming producers cull these logs for information on how their streaming content is used. You can then hone your message strategy further by discovering what resonates with your audience.

Global delivery—Radio and television signals are limited geographically. Even large broadcast networks are limited by geography and international boundaries. Individual satellites cover only part of the globe. But any computer in any country on any continent can view your audio or video stream as long as it's connected to the Internet. Geographic and political boundaries become as porous as cheesecloth.

Use network infrastructure more efficiently—Offering downloads is still a popular way to distribute media files, and it may be right for you. However, downloading, especially in high-traffic situations, could clog your network and slow down all your other Internet-dependent business processes. Streaming media systems manage the use of your network bandwidth and other resources in a way that won't negatively affect other Internet-related activities.

Here are some common uses of streaming media. This list assumes you're working in an organization that divides its audience into people outside the organization and those inside the organization:

- External audiences
  - Online radio stations
  - Market analyst calls
  - Movie trailers
  - Entertainment videos
  - Infomercials
  - Virtual tours of real estate
- Internal audiences
  - Private access to industry conferences
  - Executive communications
  - Employee training
  - Product demonstrations

One of the fun things about technology is invention. See if you can come up with a new application of streaming that will sweep the globe!

Layout and Organization of This Book

This book is organized to make your initial foray into streaming media as easy and efficient as possible. We've included three to five key terms you should know at the beginning of each chapter. Critical procedures are put into step-by-step format. Ideally, you'll be able to complete a task by following these procedures exactly. However, you should note that streaming technology changes rapidly, so be ready to adapt. The book offers some notes specifically for home users and hobbyists, so you won't feel bogged down in irrelevant information. We've also included some "expert articles" by streaming professionals to give some different perspectives on critical issues. Most of all, we ask that you take your time, let yourself make mistakes, and have some fun. If you're not having fun, there isn't much point in this streaming stuff, is there?

1 Get Started

Terms to Know

Player: A media player is a type of software installed on a desktop computer that is used to play audio or video files transmitted by a streaming media server or web server. Media players can also play files from a computer hard drive.

Metafile: A metafile is a small file on a web server containing information (metadata) that allows a media player to locate a file on a streaming media server.

Encoder: An encoder is software installed on a desktop computer (client) or server that transforms a source media file, often in **WAV, AVI,** or **MOV** format, into a file that can be streamed efficiently.

FTP Client: Software on a client or server computer that uses File Transfer Protocol (FTP) to upload to or download files from another computer at a remote location.

Fire Drill! And You're the Firefighter

How many times have you been in a situation like this: 4:45 p.m. 15 minutes to freedom. You've checked the box scores on the newspaper website. You're yearning for a sip of a cold one and a foot-long hot dog with mustard, relish, and onions, in your seat about 10 rows above first base. Just then the phone buzzes. "Jones," your boss says. "Jones, whadya know about streaming media?" Your windpipe contracts to the diameter of a pencil. You've heard about it, but you don't know a lot of details. "Well?" your boss says. "I'm leaving for XtraMegaINFOcon and I need to show we're up on streaming media. Can you put that marketing video on the website tonight?"

"But..." you start to plead.

"Thanks, Jones. You're a team player." Your boss hangs up. You hang your head. No game tonight.

Read this chapter and you can still make the game. We'll take you step-by-step through an elemental procedure for putting a streaming file on your website—fast. We'll teach you the basics about streaming media players, including where to find them and how to install them. We'll also install an encoder, which transforms raw computer audio and video files into files optimized for streaming.

Then we'll encode a file and put it on your media server. Finally, we'll write a metafile and put that on your web server. The metafile is basically a pointer to your streaming file. Confused already? Not to worry! As the great mystics say, "Be patient, and all will be revealed to you."

We won't cut corners. We'll do it right the first time, so that you'll be able to build on this knowledge in later chapters. But we'll have to make some assumptions about your resources for this chapter to make sense. Here's a list of those assumptions:

- You have a source audio or video file in a "raw" format, i.e., a file with the extension `.wav`, `.avi`, or `.mov`.
- If you choose to use Flash MX, you are familiar with the basics of creating Flash animations.
- You are familiar with the basics of using an FTP client.
- You have access to a streaming media server.
- You are allowed to upload files to a streaming server and a web server.
- You have basic knowledge of HTML.

Along with the above assumptions, we'll also ignore a couple of important streaming media caveats. We have a fire to put out. Let's get started now!

> *Home users and hobbyists:* Most of the information in this chapter is relevant to everyone involved in streaming media. However, don't be put off if some of the language seems directed at people in business situations. Just skip over it if it doesn't seem to apply to you.

What Is a Media Player?

Devices to play recorded media have been around since Thomas Edison invented the phonograph in 1877. The phonograph is essentially a media player. It transforms sound encoded in the hills and valleys of a groove etched on a metal or wax drum (the media) into pressure waves we hear as music or speech. The same goes for a cassette tape deck or a CD player. They just use different media. The term "media player" or "player" in the context of streaming media refers to a piece of software that transforms digital signals transmitted over a computer network into pressure waves and/or patterns of light and color. We interpret these waves and changes in light patterns as sound coming from a speaker or video displayed on a monitor. The technologies may be more than a century apart, but the fundamental principle is the same, as shown in Figure 1.1.

Figure 1.1 Media players date back to the 19th century. They may each use different media, but the principle behind them is the same.

Find Your Media Player

Let's first check to see if you have a media player installed on your computer. The streaming media market is dominated by four companies: RealNetworks, Microsoft, Apple Computer, and Macromedia. They make media players under the names, "RealPlayer," "Windows Media Series," "QuickTime," and "Flash." If your computer is three years old or less, there's a very good chance you have at least one and possibly two of these players already installed. If you're not sure, take a few minutes to browse your computer's hard drive for one of the players listed above.

Update Your Media Player

Let's assume you have at least one of the four major media players on your computer. The most likely suspects are RealPlayer, Windows Media, QuickTime, and Flash. Depending on the age of your computer, the particular version of your player may be pretty old. To avoid problems with outdated players, it's a good idea to upgrade your player to the latest version. The simplest way to do this is via the player's Update command. To do this, start your player and look for the command in the Help menu, as shown in the following figures.

Navigating the Marketing Shoals

When you run the Update command, you may have to navigate through a bunch of marketing messages. The software companies want you to buy players with more features or special services, and these messages can be annoying. But if you patiently click the "No, thanks" buttons, your player will eventually start the update process. And you can rest assured that the free player will play any kind of file that a "fee-based" player can.

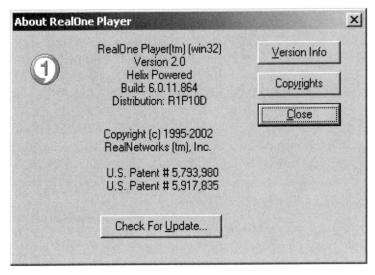

Figure 1.2   RealNetworks' RealPlayer update button under Help->About.

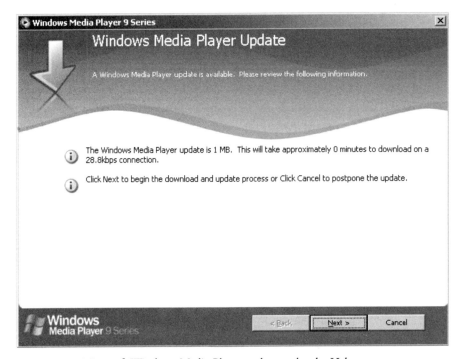

Figure 1.3   Microsoft Windows Media Player update under the Help menu.

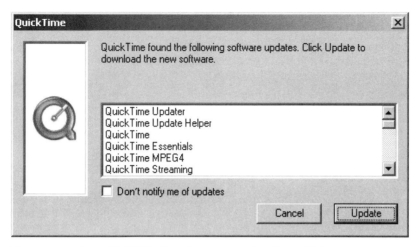

Figure 1.4 Apple QuickTime's update command under its Help menu.

A Note about Flash

Flash is slightly different than the other major media players, as it's actually a "plug-in" for your web browser. It works within your browser behind the scenes to play media streams. Unlike the other vendors, there's no stand-alone Flash player. There's also a nearly 100% chance the Flash player is already installed on your system. To upgrade your Flash player, see the list of media player download pages below, and use the Macromedia Flash Player link.

Prepare to Install a New Media Player

Okay, you've upgraded a player already installed on your machine, but you want to hedge your bets. So let's install another media player. In fact, you can install all four major media players on one machine. But beware: The major software vendors are extremely competitive. You may get messages during the installation process that ask you to prefer one player over another. There may also be other messages that suggest changes to certain settings. None of the changes will harm your computer. But read the messages carefully and make the decision you are most comfortable with.

Hardware and Software Requirements

If your computer is relatively new, you may have all the power you need to get good performance out of a new player. Here's a rule of thumb: If your computer is less than three years old, you're probably safe with what you have. But let's take a moment to look at some suggested hardware and software requirements before

Table 1.1.   Minimum and recommended hardware and software requirements for good performance by streaming media players

Minimum Requirements	Pentium II processor
	64MB of RAM
	56Kbps modem
	16-bit sound card and speakers
	65,000 color video display
	Microsoft Windows 98 or later
	Microsoft Internet Explorer 5.0 or later
Recommended Requirements	Pentium III processor
	128 MB of RAM
	Cable/DSL connection or better
	16-bit sound card and speakers
	65,000 color video display
	Microsoft Windows 98SE or later
	Internet Explorer 5.0 or later

installing a new player from scratch, as shown in Table 1.1. If you're unsure about your installed hardware and software, see your information technology (IT) support person or call a computer retailer.

Check for Restrictions

Some businesses and other organizations restrict the types of software you can download and install on your system. Check with your IT department before downloading and installing any software discussed in this book.

Websites for Players

We use free software whenever possible in this book. You should never have to pay a dime when you go to the following websites to download a new player. However, as we noted earlier, the software vendors may direct you to fee-based products or services that require entering a credit card number. (Even with free downloads, you may be asked to provide information, such as your name and address. You'll have to give it to them to get your free download. But you shouldn't need to give them a credit number.) It's annoying, but hey, they gotta make a living, too. Be persistent as you click around. You'll find the free download link eventually.

Does "Free" Mean Free?

You may see or hear the term "free software" thrown about in other contexts. What these folks really mean is "open source." In this case, "free" has nothing to do with cost. If you're curious about this and would like more information, take a quick look at the section on open source software in Chapter 5.

Here's a list of media player download pages:

- RealNetworks—http://www.realnetworks.com/info/freeplayer/
- Microsoft—http://www.microsoft.com/windows/windowsmedia/9series/player.aspx
- Apple Computer—http://www.apple.com/quicktime/products/qt/(Use the "QuickTime Player" link.)
- Macromedia—http://www.macromedia.com/downloads/(Look for the "Macromedia Flash Player" link.)

Download and Install a New Player

The following procedures detail the steps for downloading and installing media players from RealNetworks, Microsoft, Apple Computer, and Macromedia.

Backup, Backup, Backup

If you're anxious about whether all this downloading and installing could break something on your computer, save any work you have, and perform a normal backup of your critical files before starting these procedures. If you don't have a backup procedure, this is a great time to create one!

RealPlayer

Progressive Networks, now called RealNetworks, introduced the first commercially popular streaming media player in 1995. "RealAudio" and "RealVideo" are among the most recognizable streaming media brands on the Internet.

Procedure for downloading:

1. Point your web browser to http://www.realnetworks.com/info/freeplayer/
2. Click the download link appropriate for your operating system.
3. Depending on your browser, you may get a warning that asks, "Do you want to install and run RealPlayer installer?" Click Yes. The installer will do the rest.
4. If you get an error message, click the "Restart Download" button on the RealPlayer installer confirmation page.
5. If you are asked how to handle your download, click Save and put the file in a place where you can find it. Note the file name so you can locate it later. The installer file is very large, so go and fill your coffee cup while waiting for the download to complete.

Temporary Storage

We recommend creating a "Temp" directory on your hard drive for installers. It'll make it easy to find the installers, if you need to. It's also a good idea to keep a folder with all the installers you download in case you need to reinstall.

6. When the download is complete, find the folder containing the installer and double-click the icon or file name (or single click on a Mac).
7. Check "Express Install" in the Install Wizard.
8. Click Next.
9. Read the Licensing Agreement and click Accept.
10. Select the correct value for your Internet connection speed.
11. Click Finish to complete the installation.

You may be asked to fill out a form asking for your email address and other information. Unfortunately, you can't skip this step. So be careful what information you provide. You may also be asked about "Premium" or "Basic" services. Premium usually means you have to buy them with a credit card. Basic most often means free of charge.

Windows Media Series 9 Player

More Windows Media Players are installed on computers than any other player. (Some companies, notably RealNetworks, will dispute this.) Microsoft has recently started selling "premium" content services, although it has avoided trying to sell juiced-up players, at least so far.

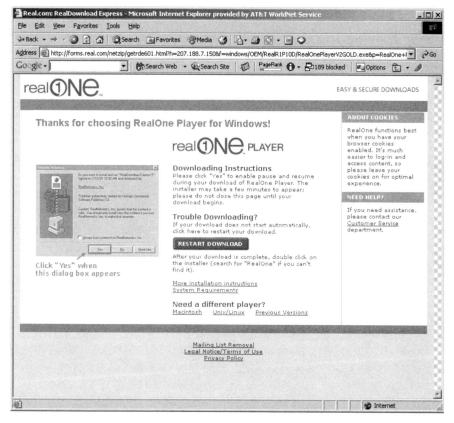

Figure 1.5   RealPlayer installer confirmation page.

Procedure for downloading:

1. Point your web browser to http://www.microsoft.com/windows/windowsmedia/9series/player.aspx

2. Click the download link appropriate for your operating system. Mac users: *Be careful.* You may have to download an earlier version of the Windows Media Player, depending on what operating system is installed on your computer.

3. If you are asked how to handle your download, click Save and put the file in a place where you can find it. Note the file name for future reference. Then take a break and wait for the installer to download.

4. Find the installer on your system and double-click it (or single click on a Mac).

5. Read the "Supplemental End User License Agreement" and click "I Accept."

Figure 1.6 RealPlayer immediately after installation. (The actual listings you see may be different than these.)

6. Read the text carefully on the next screen and click Next.
7. Review the "Privacy Options" and click Next. (You're safe using the defaults.)
8. Review the installation options and click Next. (Defaults are fine.)

QuickTime Player

The QuickTime file format (`.mov`) is one of the granddaddies of streaming media technology. However, Apple has lagged behind the industry leaders, RealNetworks and Microsoft, in deploying its streaming technology into the marketplace.

Procedure for downloading:

1. Point your web browser to http://www.apple.com/quicktime/products/qt/

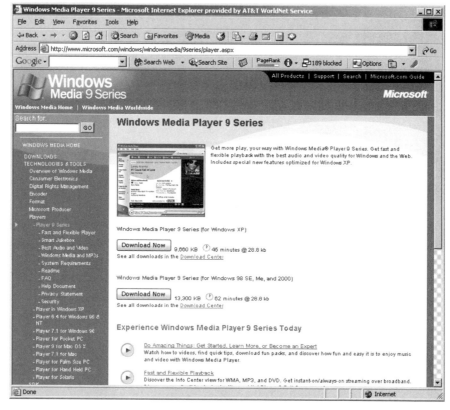

Figure 1.7   Windows Media Player 9 Series download page. Note the Mac links in the left navigation column.

2. Click the "QuickTime" download link on the page.

3. Select the option for your operating system and fill in the form.

4. You can choose to let the install happen automatically, or you can click the "download" link and save the installer to your hard drive.

5. If you choose the latter, click Save and put the file in a place where you can find it. Note the file name for future reference. You'll see that the installer is very small. This is normal for QuickTime.

6. Close any open programs before continuing.

7. When the download is complete, find the folder containing the installer and double-click it (or single click on a Mac).

8. At the "Welcome to QuickTime" screen, click Next.

9. At the second "Welcome to QuickTime" screen, click Next.

10. Read the License Agreement. Click Agree.

11. Note the destination directory for your QuickTime installation. Click Next.

Figure 1.8   Windows Media Player 9 Series player.

12. In the "Choose Installation Type" dialog box, select "Recommended" and click Next.

13. Note the Program Folder name, and click Next.

14. If you have a QuickTime 6 Pro registration number (which you probably don't), enter it here, along with other requested information. Click Next.

15. The installer will tell you it's about to download a large amount of files. Click Continue, and take a break!

16. Review the "Browser Plug-In" message, and click Next.

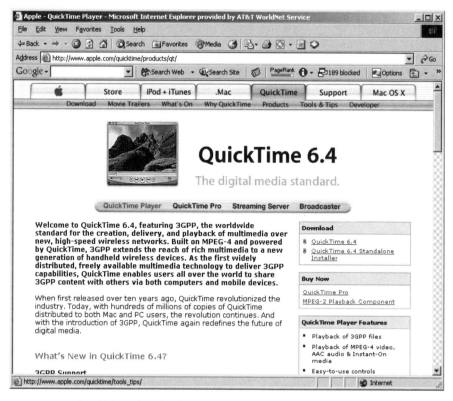

Figure 1.9 QuickTime download page.

17. Check your File Type Associations and note the extensions, such as `.aiff`. You'll learn more about these later. Click Finish.
18. Check/uncheck the boxes asking whether you'd like to read the README file and/or launch the QuickTime Player. Click Next.

Read the README file

Inexperienced computer users often ignore the README file. Don't make this mistake. READMEs can contain critical information about bugs or new features, and sometimes information about the people who made the software. Get into the habit of reading your READMEs.

A prompt may ask you whether you want to upgrade to QuickTime Pro. If you prefer the free player, click Later.

Figure 1.10 QuickTime Player.

Flash Player

Macromedia's Flash Player is the new kid on the streaming media block. But Macromedia is an old hand at tools for playing and creating online multimedia. One of the best things about Flash is the ease of installation. We wish all player installations were this easy.

Procedure for downloading:

1. Point your web browser to http://www.macromedia.com/downloads/
2. Click the "Macromedia Flash Player" download link on the page.
3. Click the "Install Now" button.
4. If you are asked whether you want to install and run "Macromedia Flash Player 6," click Yes.

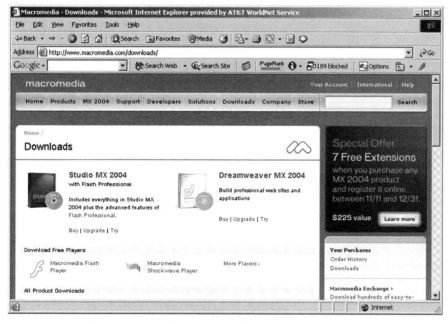

Figure 1.11 Macromedia Flash Player download page.

Note that the Flash Player is a browser plug-in, so there's no external media player to install or operate. However, if you right click over the area on the web page where the Flash Player is playing something, you may find some options to look at.

Prepare to Download and Install an Encoder

The size of audio and video files blows every other type of file out of the water. A one-minute video file can be several megabytes (that's millions of bytes), whereas a one-page letter might be only 20 or 30 kilobytes (that's thousands of bytes) in size. Trying to send enormous audio or video files using the average Internet connection is like trying to pour Niagara Falls through a garden hose. It's not going to happen.

Streaming media engineers have solved this problem with a piece of software called an "encoder," which the marketing mavens at vendors such as RealNetworks prefer to call a "producer." An encoder simply applies a mathematical formula to the original file and removes certain data while maintaining the aural and visual integrity of the original file. Encoders can shrink the original

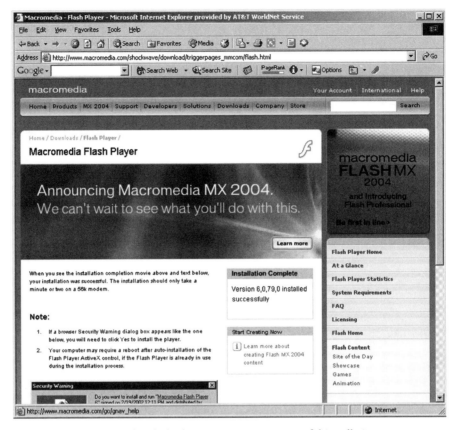

Figure 1.12   Macromedia Flash Player page noting a successful installation.

file by as much as 80 percent. Streaming media servers, the "transmitters" of streaming technology, can now send high-quality sounds and video images across the Internet much more efficiently and reliably. When you listen to or watch a well-encoded file, you can barely tell the difference from the original file. (We'll talk more about this process in Chapters 3 and 4.)

Hardware and Software Requirements

You need more processing power, memory, and storage to encode streaming media files, as opposed to simply playing them. And here's one of those assumptions we mentioned earlier: We'll assume you don't need to "capture" your audio and video from an audio or video cassette. You've been lucky enough to find your audio and video on a CD or a network hard drive in a format that we can encode (More on this later). Check Table 1.2 for our suggested minimum requirements to set up a computer for encoding.

Table 1.2. Minimum and recommended hardware and software requirements for a streaming media encoding computer

Minimum Requirements	500 MHZ Pentium II processor
	96MB of RAM
	Microsoft Windows 98SE
	500 MB hard disk space

Minimum Is the Bare Minimum

Note that the hard disk recommendation is the *absolute minimum* you can get away with. Even encoded files can be large, so build as much disk storage as you can.

Websites for Encoders

Like the websites we listed for players, we try to point you to free encoding software. But encoders are more complicated. The challenges of downloading and installing an encoder range from simple and cheap (read "free") to frustrating and expensive. It's an order of magnitude harder than downloading and installing a player, and you'll still have to wade through a lot of "upsell" messages. That's marketing talk for "sales pitches." Persevere, however, and you will be rewarded.

Here's a list of encoder download pages:

- RealNetworks—http://www.realnetworks.com/products/producer/basic.html
- Microsoft—http://www.microsoft.com/windows/windowsmedia/9series/encoder /default.aspx
- Apple Computer—No free encoder here. You'll simply upgrade the player to a player/encoder.
- Macromedia—No free version. But a 30-day trial version is available at http://www.macromedia.com/software/flash/

Download and Install a Media Encoder

The following procedures detail the steps for downloading and installing encoders from RealNetworks, Microsoft, Apple Computer, and Macromedia.

RealNetworks RealProducer Basic

You'll find links to free versions of its encoder, along with free versions of other RealNetworks' products, throughout the RealNetworks' website.

Procedure for downloading:

1.   Point your browser to http://www.realnetworks.com/products/producer/basic.html
2.   Look for the link to "RealProducer Basic." Click the link.
3.   Fill out the form and click Submit.
4.   Click on a location near you to begin downloading. If you want to save the installer, right click on the link and select Save Target As. Save it to a directory where you can find it later. Note the file name for future reference. As usual, the file is huge, so write your mom a nice letter while you're waiting.
5.   When the download is complete, find the folder with the installer and double-click it (Single click for Mac users).
6.   Read the License Agreement and select the acceptance radio button. Click Next.
7.   Note the install options, including the directory location of the encoder. Click Install.
8.   When the Finishing Up dialog box appears, check the options, and click Finish.
9.   The encoder will start. Spend a bit of time with it and learn your way around.

Microsoft Windows Media Encoder 9 Series

Unlike RealNetworks, Microsoft doesn't try to sell you a fancier version of its encoder.

Procedure for downloading:

1.   Point your browser to http://www.microsoft.com/windows/windowsmedia/9series/encoder/default.aspx
2.   Click the Download Now button. Save the file to an easy-to-find location, such as a temp directory or your desktop. Relax while the installer downloads. When the download is complete, find the folder with the installer and double-click it.
3.   At the welcome screen, click Next.
4.   Read the End User License Agreement. Select the acceptance button and click Next.
5.   Click Install at the next screen. Then click Finish.
6.   You may be asked to restart your computer. Do so.

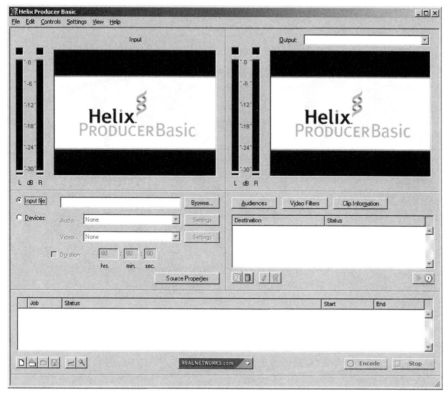

Figure 1.13 The RealNetworks RealProducer Basic after installation.

7. To start the encoder, click Start->Programs->Windows Media-> Windows Media Encoder. Spend some time getting intimate with the software.

Apple Computer QuickTime Pro

Apple is the only company that has combined its streaming media player with its encoder.

Procedure for downloading:

1. Start QuickTime Player
2. Click Edit->Preferences->Registration.
3. Click Register Online. Your browser will go to the QuickTime registration page.
4. Click the options appropriate for your system.
5. Create an account, if needed, and purchase the registration key.

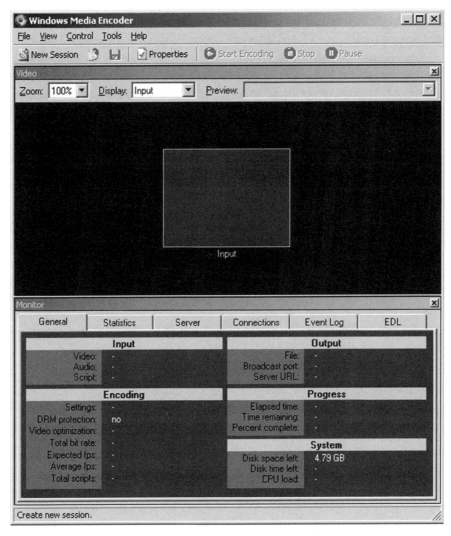

Figure 1.14 Microsoft Windows Media Encoder 9 after installation.

6. Once the purchase is completed, click the Edit Registration button on the Registration dialog box.

7. Copy and paste the key into the Registration Number text box. Click OK.

8. Close the Registration dialog box.

9. Restart QuickTime Player, which is now QuickTime Pro.

10. Click the File drop-down menu. Note the new options, including the Import and Export commands.

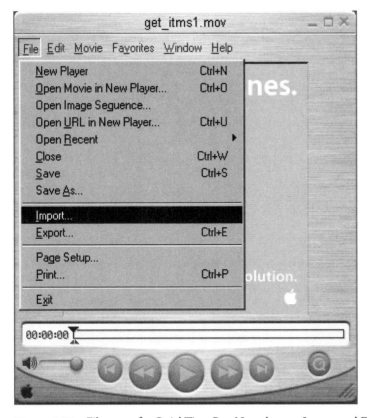

Figure 1.15 File menu for QuickTime Pro. Note the new Import and Export commands.

Macromedia Flash MX

Macromedia added streaming media capabilities to its Flash multimedia authoring system in 2002. Web designers immediately used it to embed streaming audio and video into Flash presentations. If you'd like to try Flash MX, you'll need to download and install the entire Flash authoring system, which is rather expensive and complex if you're not a multimedia authoring specialist. However, you can test the waters with the trial version of Flash MX. We'll use that for our examples.

Procedure for downloading:

1. Point your browser to http://www.macromedia.com/downloads/
2. Find the Flash MX section, and click the Try link.
3. Fill in the forms to get to the download page.
4. On the download page, select the Flash MX version that matched your system. Click the Download button, and save the file to a place where you can find it, such as your desktop. Note the file name for future

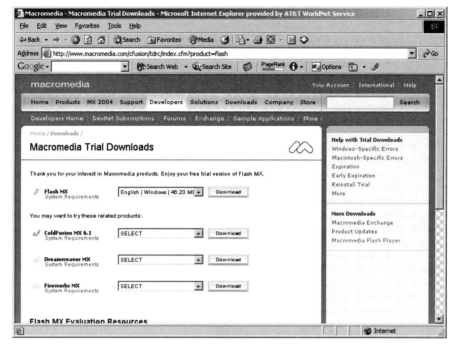

Figure 1.16   The Macromedia trial downloads page. Note the file size for the Flash MX download.

>   reference. The file size is unbelievably enormous. Always wanted to write a novel? By the time you're done writing it, the download will be almost finished.

5.   When the download is complete, find the folder with the installer and double-click it if you're on a PC, or single click it if you're on a Mac.

6.   Complete all the installation instructions.

Prepare to Encode an Audio and Video File

We need to reduce the size of our raw audio or video file so it will "fit" into the maze of data pipes called the Internet. (Remember our assumptions above: You already have your audio data in a format we can encode. In the cast of audio, that's commonly the WAV format. For video, it's commonly the AVI or MOV format. If you don't have a file to encode, and just want to learn encoding, see the first procedure below.) Now that you've downloaded and installed an encoder, it's time to encode the raw or "source" file. As we said above, an encoder applies a mathematical formula to reduce the file size, performing a procedure called "transcoding." Essentially, the formula throws away data that your brain doesn't need in order to understand the sound of Ricky Martin singing *Livin' La Vida Loca* or the image of the president giving the State of the Union address.

While you're going through these procedures, you'll see lots of potentially confusing options and terms. Ignore them and use the defaults as supplied by the vendors. They're usually good enough to get you started.

Fast WAV Tutorial

Before we start encoding an audio file, it's good to know something about the **WAV** format. The WAV format, pronounced, "wave," is the standard format for storing audio signals on the personal computer. It was invented jointed by Microsoft and IBM in the 1980s. The format can store all types of sound with virtually any quality, including stereo. You can play WAV files with dozens of applications, including most streaming media players. These audio files use the file extension `.wav`.

The main problem with `.wav` files is their size. They're just too big to stream reliably. That's why we need to encode them.

AIFF Files Work, Too

Mac users: Most of the information about .wav files can be applied to Apple Computer's sound format, known as **AIFF**. These files have the extension `.aiff` or `.aif`.

Find a WAV File to Encode

Let's say you want to learn to encode, but you don't have a `.wav` file handy. Actually, you probably have dozens of them on your personal computer, and you just don't know it. Microsoft loves to put `.wav` files on your computer for a variety of purposes. You know that "Ding!" sound you hear every time you goof? That's a `.wav` file. Let's find one for you to encode.

Procedure for finding a `.wav` file:

We'll use your operating system's search function to find a `.wav` file to play with.

1. Click Start->Search->For Files or Folders. (If you're on a Mac, use the Finder tool.)
2. In the search box, type `*.wav`. The "`*`" is a wildcard character that will allow us to find all the files with a `.wav` extension.

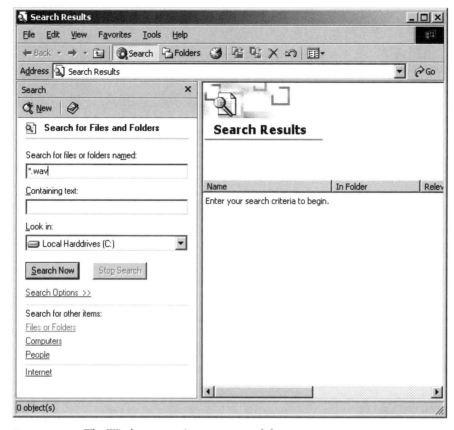

Figure 1.17   The Windows operating system search box.

3. Select your local hard drive as the drive to search.
4. Click the Search button.
5. The search will probably turn up dozens of files. Look for one that lasts at least 10 seconds when you play it, or has a large file size, say 100 to 500 kilobytes. That will give you something substantial to work with, but won't take a lot of time to encode.
6. Copy the file to a temporary or working directory.
7. Give the file a new name to distinguish it from other projects. Many people enter the project, the date, and the producer's name in the file name.

Encode a WAV File

Here are basic procedures for encoding a `.wav` file with the leading proprietary streaming media encoders.

Procedure for encoding using RealNetworks RealProducer Basic:

1. Start the RealProducer Basic.
2. Select File->Open Input File.
3. Find your audio file, select it, and click Open.
4. Click Encode.
5. Look in your working directory for the newly encoded file. It will have the same name, but with a new extension, `.rm`.
6. Double click the file to play it.

Procedure for encoding using Microsoft Windows Media Series Encoder:

1. Start the Windows Media Series Encoder.
2. Click Convert a File wizard in the wizards option box.
3. Use the Browse button to find your source audio file, select it, and click Open. Note the directory location for the output file. Click Next.

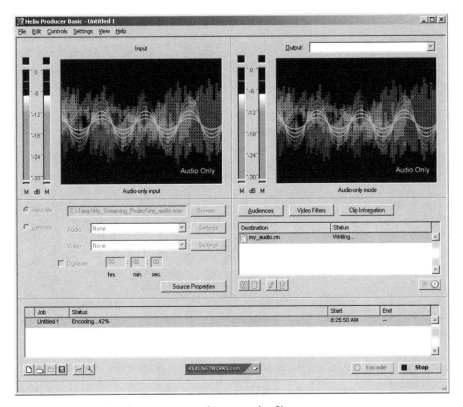

Figure 1.18 RealProducer Basic encoding an audio file.

4. In the Content Distribution dialog box, click Windows Media Server.

5. In the Encoding Options window, look for the Bit Rate area. Scroll down and check the 19 Kbps (kilobytes per second) option in the Total Bit Rate column. Uncheck all other options. Click Next.

6. In the Display Information dialog, fill in the form. (You can skip this step, if you like.) Click Next.

7. In the Settings Review dialog box, click Finish.

8. When the encoding is complete, click Close.

9. Look in your working directory for the newly encoded file with the extension `.wma`. Double click the file to play it.

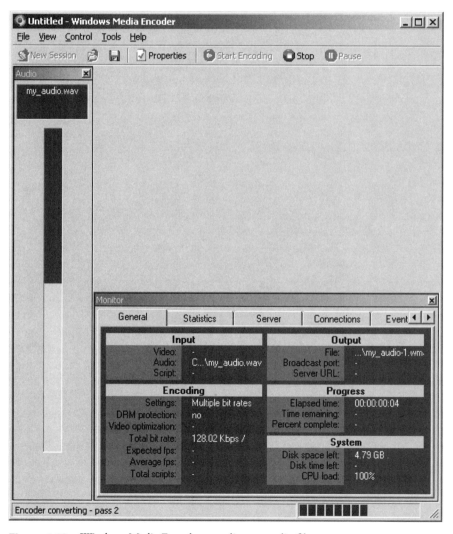

Figure 1.19 Windows Media Encoder encoding an audio file.

Apple QuickTime Pro

Apple's Encoder

Apple Computer does not have a free encoder. You will need to purchase a QuickTime Pro license from Apple Computer to use the QuickTime encoding features.

Procedure for encoding using QuickTime Pro:

1. Start QuickTime Pro.
2. Select File->Import File.
3. Find your working directory.
4. In the Files of Type drop-down menu, select Audio Files.
5. Select your audio file, and click Convert. A new QuickTime Player window opens.
6. In the new window, select File->Export File.
7. In the Save Exported File As window, select your `.wav` file.
8. In the Export drop-down menu, select the Movie to QuickTime Movie option. (Even though this is an audio file, QuickTime Pro treats it as a "movie.")
9. Click Save.
10. Look in your working directory for the newly encoded file with the extension `.mov`. That's the QuickTime Movie extension. Double click the file to play it.

Procedure to encode using Macromedia Flash MX:

1. Start Flash MX.
2. Create a new animation project.
3. Create an audio layer.
4. Select File->Import to Library and find your audio file in your working directory. Click Open. Your audio file is now added to your Library.
5. Select a Key Frame for the audio.
6. In the Properties panel, click the Sound drop-down menu and select your audio file.
7. In the Properties panel, click the Sync drop-down menu and select Stream.
8. Click File->Publish Settings and select the Flash (`.swf`) Type. Give the file a name.
9. Click on the Flash Tab. Make sure Compress Movie is checked.
10. Click Publish.

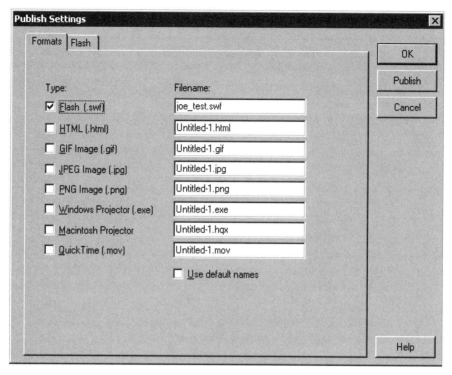

Figure 1.20   Macromedia Flash MX Publish settings.

11.   A file with the .swf extension will be created in the directory where you normally publish (save) your .swf files. To play the file, open it with your Web browser. Remember, Flash is played via a plug-in in your browser.

Fast AVI Tutorial

Source video files come in several different formats. But we're going to stick with the most common, called AVI, which stands for "Audio Video Interleaved." It's the most common one on the personal computer. (The MOV file is the most common on a Mac. For now, we'll just use AVI.) AVI files have the extension .avi. Like .wav files, you can play .avi files, and even stream them to your media player. But AVIs are among the single largest files in the known universe. And that's why we have to encode them to fit them into the Internet.

Find an AVI File

You can try the operating system search trick we used above for finding a .wav file if you don't already have a video file to play with. Unfortunately, there aren't many .avi files on a typical hard drive. (One reason why: file size.) However, you can find public domain `.avi` files on the Internet for experimenting. The NASA archives at the NASA website is a good place to look at http://www.nasa.gov. We downloaded an AVI file of President John F. Kennedy announcing his intention to send a man to the moon.

Encode an AVI File

These are the procedures for encoding an AVI file with the leading proprietary streaming media encoders.

Procedure to encode an AVI file using RealNetworks RealProducer Basic:

1. Start the RealProducer Basic.
2. Select File->Open Input File.
3. Find your video file, select it, and click Open.
4. Click Encode.

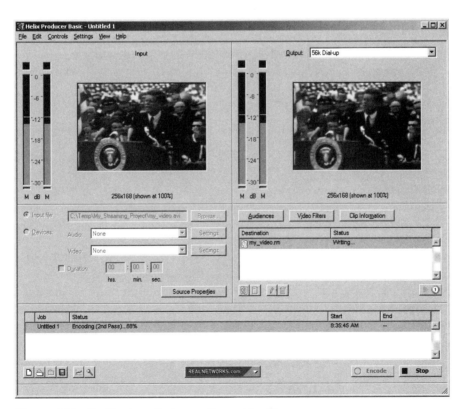

Figure 1.21 RealProducer Basic encoding a video file.

5. Open your working directory and look for the newly encoded file, which will have the file extension `.rm`. Double click the file to play it.

Procedure to encode an AVI file using Microsoft Windows Media Series Encoder:

1. Start the Windows Media Series Encoder.
2. Click Convert a File wizard in the wizards option box.
3. Use the Browse button to find your source video file, select it, and click Open. Note the directory location for the output file. Click Next.
4. In the Content Distribution dialog box, click Windows Media Server.
5. In the Encoding Options window, look for the Bit Rate area. Scroll down and uncheck the 292 Kbps option and check the 43 Kbps option in the Total Bit Rate column. (We'll explain the meaning of "bit rate" in later chapters.) Click Next.
6. In the Display Information dialog box, fill in the form (optional). Click Next.
7. In the Settings Review dialog box, click Finish.
8. When the encoding is complete, click Close.
9. You'll find a new file in your working directory with the `.wmv` extension. Double click the file to play it.

Procedure to encode an AVI file using Apple QuickTime Pro:

1. Start QuickTime Pro.
2. Select File->Import File.
3. Find your working directory.
4. Select your video file, and click Convert. A new QuickTime Player window opens.
5. In the new window, select File->Export File.
6. In the Save Exported File As window, select your `.avi` file.
7. In the Export drop-down menu, select the Movie to QuickTime Movie option.
8. In the Use drop-down menu, select Default Settings.
9. Click Save.
10. Look in your working directory for the newly encoded file with the extension `.mov`. That's the QuickTime Movie extension. Double click the file to play it.

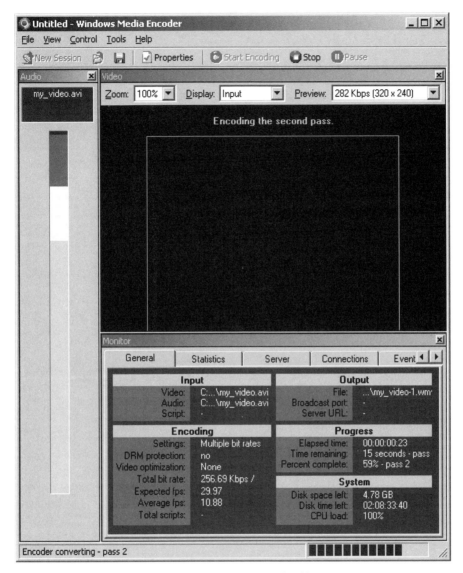

Figure 1.22   Windows Media Encoder encoding a video file.

Procedure to encode an AVI file using Macromedia Flash MX:

1. Start Flash MX.
2. Open your animation project.
3. Select File->Import and find your video file in your working directory. Click Open.
4. In the Import Video window, select "Embed video in Macromedia Flash document." Click OK.
5. In the Import Video Settings, click OK.

Build a Play/Pause Button

In the following section, we'll assume that you have built a play/pause button for your video using Flash MX animation tools. We make this assumption because Flash doesn't automatically include these features when you create a streaming video. The other vendors' media players already have these VCR-like buttons.

6.   You may be asked to let Flash MX increase the number of frames to the length required. Click OK.
7.   In the Properties panel, click the Sync drop-down menu. Select Stream.
8.   In the File menu, select Publish Settings. In the Format tab, select the Flash (`.swf`) type. Give the file a unique name.
9.   Click Publish.
10. Look in your working directory for a file with the `.swf` extension, sometimes pronounced "swiff." Drag and drop this file into your Web browser to play it.

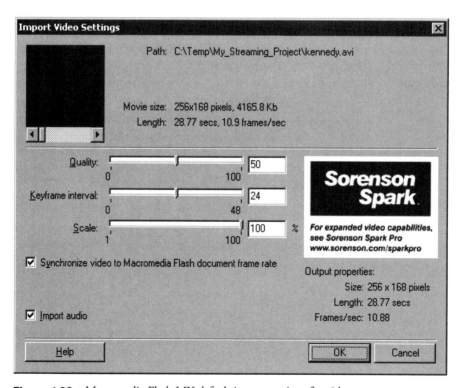

Figure 1.23   Macromedia Flash MX default import settings for video.

Put the Newly Encoded Media File on Your Streaming Server

We're now going to dive into one of the major facets of streaming: serving. You've probably heard or even worked with a web server, which is software specifically designed to send text files, graphics, and other kinds of files to web browsers. Web servers can also serve encoded media files, but not very efficiently or reliably. Streaming media files are served by streaming media servers, which are specially designed to send files that depend on a timeline.

Media files differ from other kinds of files. Sound and video change over time, unlike the picture of your grandmother on your personal web page. This means the player and the server need to communicate with each other while the media file is playing. For example, data can get lost as it traverses the Internet. This could manifest as an audio dropout or a missed video frame. To maintain a good user experience, the player needs to keep in touch with the server to make sure it hasn't lost any data. It may request the lost data again, if needed. In contrast, when a web browser requests information, the web server just sends it off and forgets about it.

To prepare for the next step in putting a streaming file on your website, let's recall three of our assumptions from the beginning of this chapter, namely that (1) You know how to use an FTP client, (2) You have access to a streaming media server, and (3) You have permission to put files on your streaming server.

Get an FTP Client

An FTP (File Transfer Protocol) client is software that helps you manage uploads and downloads from any kind of server. You've probably downloaded files using your web browser. But most people upload files with an FTP client. (Uploading with web browsers is awkward.) We're not going to teach you how to use an FTP client. But if you need to install FTP software on your computer, here are a few to try:

- WS_FTP LE—Probably the most popular FTP desktop client. "LE" is the free version. http://www.ipswitch.com/downloads/index.html
- FTP Commander—A basic, no-frills client. http://www.internet-soft.com/ftpcomm.htm
- Cute FTP—Another basic client. http://www.cuteftp.com/cuteftp/

Find Your Media Server

Now is the time to get to know your network administrator. This is the individual who keeps your company, school, or home connected to the Internet. You are completely dependent on this person. Do not annoy him or her. If you do, it will haunt you forever and make your life a living hell (only a slight exaggeration). To avoid this, humbly approach the network administrator with your problem. Politely explain that you have been asked to put a streaming media file on your organization's streaming media server, and that you have already encoded the file. Indicate the size of the encoded file.

"Do we have a streaming server?" you ask the administrator. There's a very good chance the answer is "Yes," especially in the case of Windows Media Series 9 or RealNetworks' platform. The Windows Media server is bundled with other Microsoft networking products and may have never been used. This is a chance for your network administrator to get more value out of your company's investment in networking products.

To use RealNetworks' platform, the network administrator must download and install the server. RealNetworks offers a free basic server that's painless to install and set up. The administrator may have to deal with issues such as firewalls, DMZs, bandwidth allocation, and other networking guru stuff. (The same goes for any other media server.) But it can be done with relatively little effort. Convince him or her that helping you ultimately enhances his or her position as well as the company's.

You will also need access to the organization's web server, and the administrator will need to set up an account for you. The same goes for the streaming server, which ideally lives on a separate computer. When you get back to your desk, test your streaming server FTP account and upload a small file. If all goes well with this test, go ahead and upload your streaming file. (You'll be working with the web server in a minute.)

Here are the steps required to put your encoded streaming file on your streaming server:

1. Open your FTP client program.
2. Connect to your media server. The network administrator will show you how to do this.
3. Locate your encoded file on your local computer or network drive.
4. Upload the encoded file.
5. Note the location (i.e., the path, of your encoded file on the media server).
6. Test the file by playing it from your media server. We'll use Windows Media Player as the example, but the process is virtually the same for RealPlayer and QuickTime Player.
7. Start Windows Media Player.
8. Click File->Open URL.
9. In the dialog box, type the following location, substituting the appropriate information for your network: mms://www.yourcompany.com:1755/yourpath/yourfile.wmv
10. Click OK.

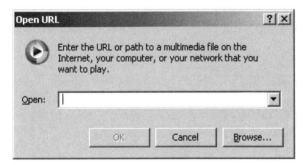

Figure 1.24   Windows Media Player Open URL dialog box.

The Real Protocol

Whether you're using a RealNetworks Helix Server or another server, the first three or four letters of the URL, known as the protocol, are usually "rtsp," "mms," or "http." Check with your network administrator for the correct protocol to use.

Watch carefully for error messages. The most common is some variation of "file not found." Check your notes and call the network administrator if you're unsure what to do. If all goes well, your file will start playing. Congratulations! Don't forget to send your network administrator a nice thank you note.

Flash MX users: No, we haven't forgotten you. In this book, we won't use a streaming server for Flash files. (Macromedia sells a streaming server for Flash files, but it's not widely used, compared to the other vendors.) Instead, most people put Flash audio and video files on a web server, and you should do the same for now. Upload your Flash files to your web server, and test them by playing them through your web browser. The URL will begin with "http."

Prepare to Create a Metafile

When you click a link on a web page, the browser contacts the web server and requests the page you want to look at. A link to streaming media works a little differently. Instead of linking directly to your newly uploaded media file, you have to build an intermediate step using something called a "metafile." The "meta" prefix, especially in computer applications, most often refers to data that describe or relate to other data. A streaming media metafile describes a media file in terms of its location on the streaming server. It's all very confusing. But we'll work through it, step-by-step.

Web Servers vs. Media Servers

Web servers are one of the core pieces of Internet software. They are fairly simple networking applications. When you click a link in a browser, the browser sends a request via the HyperText Transfer Protocol (HTTP) to the web server, which responds by sending the requested HyperText Markup Language (HTML) file to the requesting browser, along with associated graphics and text. There are a few other important features of web servers, such as their ability to respond to requests for encrypted information. But that's the extent of it.

Media servers, on the other hand, are more complex and specialized. Unlike a web server, a media server stays in constant contact with the media player while it delivers a media file. The media server uses a variety of protocols, including HTTP, to deliver the media file to the player and manage its progress. And because of the huge amounts of data involved, most media servers are designed to manage player connections and bandwidth consumption better than web servers.

In fact, you should determine whether your organization or Internet service provider (ISP) runs its media server on a separate computer. Most media server vendors recommend that media servers run on a separate computer because of their specialized nature. That leads to the need for a metafile.

Metafiles and Media Players

A streaming media metafile is a small text file containing the location of the encoded audio or video file on the streaming media server. The location is stored as a URL, which points to the streaming media server. The link on a web page meant to show an audio or video file points to this metafile. When the link is clicked, the web server delivers the metafile to the browser, which hands the file to the correct media player on the user's computer. The media player opens the metafile, loads the URL, and requests audio/video data from the streaming server, that is, it plays the file.

The Why of Metafiles

Why are metafiles necessary? Some web browsers don't understand how to communicate with streaming media servers. Metafiles avoid this problem by telling the browser to hand the streaming file to a media player.

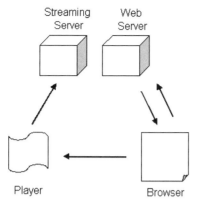

Figure 1.25   How the browser, media player, web server, and streaming server work together.

For this process to work, you will need to write a metafile and place it on your web server.

Write a Metafile

Metafiles range from very simple to highly complex. They can simply point to an audio or video file, or they can set all kinds of parameters. We're going to keep things as simple as possible. But as usual, different vendors implement the metafile model differently. First, we'll list common steps for all the vendors. Then, we'll go through the vendors one by one.

Common Metafile Creation Steps

Here are metafile creation steps common to all major streaming media systems:

1. Make note of the location of your encoded file on your media server. Remember the test above where you played the file directly through the media player? The URL that goes in the metafile is exactly the same. If you're having trouble, speak to your IT support staff or network administrator.
2. Open a new file in a text editor such as Notepad or SimpleText. (Avoid word-processing programs such as Microsoft Word. Files created or modified by word processors incorporate hidden code that can confuse media players.)
3. Copy the media file URL from the Open URL (or similar) dialog box in your media player.
4. Paste this information into the open text file.
5. Save the text file with the appropriation extension.
6. Upload the new metafile to your web server.

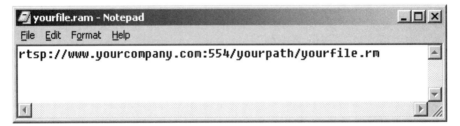

Figure 1.26   A media file URL pasted into a new text file and saved with an appropriate extension, in this case, `.ram` for RealAudio or RealVideo.

Mind Your MIME Types

The file extension, that is, the last two or three characters of a file after the dot, is a critical part of the interaction between browser and media player. When the browser requests and downloads the metafile, it looks at this extension to determine which media player should handle the file. The extension is associated with a "MIME type," a standard way of classifying a file distributed over the Internet. For example, the video MIME type associated with the QuickTime format extension `.mov` is video/quicktime. By the way, MIME stands for Multi-purpose Internet Mail Extensions.

We'll now go through each of the vendors' implementations.

RealNetworks' RealPlayer/Helix

1. Note the URL to your media file on the streaming media server.
2. Open a new text file with a text editor.
3. Write or copy/paste the URL in the text file. Your line will look something like this: rtsp://www.yourcompany.com:554/pathtofile/filename.rm
4. Save the text file with the extension .ram. This extension identifies the file as a metafile for the RealNetworks system.
5. Upload the text file to your web server with your FTP client and note the file's location for future reference.

Testing Your Metafiles

To test metafiles for any vendors' system, type the location of the metafile on your web server in the location bar of your web browser and click Go or hit Enter. For example, your location might be: http://www.yourcompany.com/pathtometafile/mymetafile.ram

   If you get a "file not found" error from your browser, check the location again. If the media player starts, but it gives you a "file not found" error, then the URL in the metafile is wrong. If you fix these things and still have problems, see your network administrator and show him or her the error message.

Microsoft Windows Media Series 9

1. Note the URL to your media file on the streaming media server.
2. Open a new text file with a text editor.
3. Copy the following code *exactly* into the text file.
   ```
   <ASX version = "3.0">
     <Entry>
       <Ref href = "[placeholder]" />
     </Entry>
   </ASX>
   ```
4. Replace the text "[placeholder]" with the URL to your audio or video on your streaming server. (Keep the quotes.) The URL may look something like this: mms://www.yourcompany.com:1755/yourpath/yourfile.wmv
5. Save the text file with the extension `.asx`. This extension identifies the file as a metafile for the Windows Media system.
6. Upload the text file to your web server with your FTP client and note the file's location for future reference.

Apple QuickTime

1. Ask your network administrator whether the MIME type "application/x-quicktimeplayer" is included in your web server's MIME type lookup table. If so, it should be associated with the `.qtl` file extension. Your network administrator will need to add this information if it isn't in the lookup table in order for QuickTime streaming to work.

2. Note the URL to your media file on the streaming media server.
3. Start QuickTime Pro 6.
4. Select Open Movie in New Player and select your encoded file.
5. From the File menu, select Export.
6. Find your encoded QuickTime file and select it.
7. In the Export drop-down menu, select "Movie to QuickTime Media Link." Note that the file now has the `.qtl` extension. If it does not, change the file extension to `.qtl` to avoid overwriting your encoded media file.
8. Click the Options button to open the QuickTime Media Link Settings dialog box.
9. In the URL field, type the URL to your file on your streaming server.
10. Click OK.
11. Click Save.
12. Upload the metafile to your web server with your FTP client and note the file's location.

Macromedia Flash MX

We're going to stream our Flash MX audio and video files directly off the web server, despite our earlier advice to separate streaming from web serving. Therefore, we don't need a metafile. Just upload your Flash MX file to the web server and note its location.

Prepare to Link to Your Metafile via Your Web Page

The last step is creating a link in your web page to your metafile. Now is a great time to meet your web designer/developer and explain what you're doing. (Actually, you probably should've given him or her a heads up at the beginning of this process.) Or you may have direct access to your organization's web pages. You almost certainly have access to your personal web pages. If you haven't worked with an HTML page for a while, you might refresh your memory with an HTML tutorial or instruction book.

Build a Link to Your Metafile in Your Web Page

Here is some very simple code for linking to your metafile. It actually creates an entire, small, web page. You can adapt this code to your specific needs.

```
<html>
  <body>
  <a href="http://www.yourcompany.com/pathtometafile/mymetafile.XXX"/>
Audio/Video</a>
  </body>
</html>
```

Important! Don't forget to replace the XXX with the correct file extension for your metafile, such as `.ram`. It doesn't have to be capitalized. Finally, upload the modified web page to your web server, load it into your browser, and test the link.

Congratulations! You have put out the fire!

Chapter Summary

We discussed the nature of streaming media players and installed players from the leading vendors. We also went over the basic principles of encoding and installed encoders from the leading vendors. We took you through the steps of encoding an audio or video file into popular streaming media formats. You learned the difference between a web server and a streaming server. You wrote a metafile pointing to your encoded media file and placed the metafile on your web server. Finally, you included HTML code in your web pages that links to your metafile. In the next chapter, we'll go back to the beginning and discuss the processes and tools you need in order to capture audio and video.

How I Got Started in Streaming Media

By Joe Follansbee

Beginnings excite people. When something starts, such as a football game, a spring day, a new life, the future seems limitless.

That's how I felt when I first learned about streaming media. In the spring of 1995, I was a community journalist. I wrote and produced radio news reports for the Minnesota Public Radio station in Rochester. I talked with city council members, chatted with police officers, interviewed business owners, and recorded elementary school children. I brought their information back to my studio and crafted audio stories about the people of Rochester and the small towns of southeastern Minnesota. I had been a practicing journalist for nine years, first at an Oregon newspaper, then in public radio.

In 1995, the Internet and the World Wide Web had just begun to penetrate the public mind. Email addresses appeared on business cards. Web sites numbered about 100,000. Version 1.0 of Netscape Navigator dominated the browser market. Netscape's initial public offering (IPO) later that year heralded the 1990s stock market bubble. Minnesota

Continued

Public Radio saw the value of the Internet early on: As part of a communications strategy to link its stations all around the state, it had added web access in 1994.

I browsed the Net with my office computer, which ran DOS on an Intel 286 processor, already ancient in 1995. I was captivated by the ability to retrieve information from New York, Paris, Geneva, San Francisco, and Seattle in an instant. I exchanged email with people whom I would probably never meet in person, usually at other public radio stations. One day in April or May, I read an email about a new way to send sounds from one place to another, a method with no boundaries of time or space.

The email said a company in Seattle called Progressive Networks had invented something called "RealAudio." The company announced the product at the 1995 National Association of Broadcasters convention in Las Vegas. It said National Public Radio would be one of the first partners in a broadcasting revolution. Many of my public radio colleagues were alarmed. They saw RealAudio, streaming media, and the NPR partnership as an end run around local public stations, which depend on NPR for programming. Thus began one of the first arguments over control of audio content. The argument would continue in other forms, such as the Napster debate, and struggles over royalties on songs played on radio stations broadcasting over the Internet.

However, I was excited about the possibilities. I imagined broadcasters and audio artists completely released from the technical and legal boundaries of conventional radio. I could broadcast anything to anyone anywhere on the planet, all from a desktop computer in my apartment. What incredible freedom! I downloaded and installed the RealAudio 1.0 player on my new Intel 486 personal computer, which had Windows 3.1, a 250-megabyte disk drive, and 8 megabytes of RAM. I clicked the Play button, and I heard a scratchy, muffled, but understandable human voice in the 1-¼-inch computer speakers. The voice came through my 14.4 Kbps dialup connection from a server in Seattle.

I wanted to participate in the revolution. The Progressive Networks (PN) website invited RealAudio users to submit audio work to the company's online technology showcase. I convinced my boss at MPR to let me send in one of my radio stories. I picked a piece about an old jail in a tiny Minnesota town. I hooked up my Marantz portable tape deck to the sound card on my home computer, captured the audio, encoded it, and uploaded it to PN. I was certain I was competing against million-dollar Hollywood productions. I was stunned when PN accepted my story. I submitted two more, which were also accepted. Half the audio pieces on the PN showcase were my stories.

I followed PN's fortunes over the next months. I exchanged email with the PN webmaster about other contributions I could make. Near the end of 1995, I spotted a job announcement for a "Special Projects Editor." In February of 1996, I flew to Seattle and interviewed for the job. A month later, I moved my family to Seattle and started work. The company had less than 100 employees, but it was already growing out of its tiny space in a century-old downtown building. I narrowly avoided having my desk placed next to the men's room door.

That was my beginning in streaming media. RealNetworks is behind me, but I'm still excited about the technology and its potential. And the story has just begun.

2 Get Your Audio and Video Now

Terms to Know

Input: An input is analog or digital data that flows into a recording device such as a camera. Input may also refer to a physical connection that accepts data from another connector.

Output: Output refers to analog or digital data that flows away from a source, such as from one recording device to another. An output may also refer to a physical connection that sends data into an input.

Analog: The term "analog" describes data that flows in a continuous, often variable mechanical or electrical signal. Analog devices include the phonograph and early tape recorders.

Digital: Data broken into "binary" information, usually characterized as "1s" and "0s", is referred to as digital. All electronic devices designed around a computer chip, including most new designs of recording devices, are digital.

You've Put Out the Fire. Now What?

Chapter 1 helped you put out the fire started by your boss's trip to XtraMegaINFOcon. You put your feet up on your desk and bask in your boss's praise. He calls you from the conference booth and says, "Jones, the booth is packed. Everyone saw the marketing video you put up on the website and they want to see more! I want you to..."

Oh, Lord. Here it comes, you say to yourself.

"...get a new video produced and up on the site in time for the Hardware Hype and Vaporware Show next month at Circus[2] in Las Vegas. We want to make a big splash with the new product. Ok, Jones? JONES!"

You passed out for a couple of seconds, having hit your head on the floor when you fell backwards out of your chair. But you collect yourself and say, "Yes, sir," like a good soldier, and hang up.

Yep, your boss has handed you a big task. But it's definitely doable. We're going to build on many of the basic principles you learned in Chapter 1. But we'll begin with how to plan a streaming media production. Fortunately, you've got a decent budget, though it's not bottomless. We'll talk about the equipment you'll need to buy, and we'll also discuss how to get "raw" or "source" audio and video from a recording device to a workstation in preparation for more sophisticated encoding.

Throughout the rest of this book, we'll rely on the words of pioneering French chemist Louis Pasteur: "Fortune favors the prepared mind." In other words, you'll make your own good luck if you put time and energy into detailed preparation and research. We'll help you set yourself up for success.

Time Out! Can't I Just Hire Someone Else to Do This?

The short answer is, yes, you can outsource your streaming production to someone else. In fact, it might be the wisest thing to do, if your situation meets one or more of the following criteria:

- Audio and video production is not your forte.
- Your future use of streaming media will be infrequent and irregular.
- You feel comfortable shopping around for an experienced individual or team.

If you meet these criteria, visit the outsourcing section in Chapter 4. However, if you don't meet one or more of the criteria, or you're ready to expand your skill set and you have the okay from your boss, take the time to read this chapter.

Home users and hobbyists: Common sense tells us that good planning brings good results. But you don't necessarily have to write a script, come up with budgets, and scout locations if you just want to put your daughter's birthday party video online. And you don't have to buy thousands of dollars worth of equipment. The principles and hardware recommendations listed below apply primarily to media professionals.

Why Audio Is Important to Videographers

Question to author: I'm a videographer, and I see a lot of audio-only material in this chapter and the book in general. Why do I need to know about audio-only recording equipment and techniques?

The author responds: Audio-only techniques are a great introduction to streaming media basics and an excellent step toward more complex video streaming methods.

Furthermore, I believe high-quality audio is more important to successful streaming than to standard video production. In my experience, many video producers tend to focus on the "visuals" at the expense of audio quality. They love "whip" pans, fast dissolves, jump cuts, and other techniques. At the same time, they forget basic sound recording techniques, such as proper microphone setup. If you want to be a successful streaming producer, shift some of your production energy from visuals to "aurals."

I'd like you to do this experiment in your office or at home. Turn on your television (or even start a video stream), and turn off the sound for two or three minutes. Watch the video. Then turn up the sound and leave the room for two or three minutes. Stay close enough so that you can hear the sound but can't see the pictures. Compare the "with sound" minutes to the "without sound" minutes. In which case did you receive the greatest quantity and quality of information? I'll bet money it was the "with sound" minutes. People generally use the Internet to gather useful information, and it's imperative that your streams be information-driven. And since most useful information in video is actually delivered by the *audio*, paying close attention to audio quality pays off. Poor audio quality will turn Internet users away.

Pre-Production Planning

Experts have written dozens of volumes about planning audio and video productions. It's really about "risk management," that is, thinking ahead and reducing the potential for upsetting surprises. We're focused on the streaming media part, but it's worth reviewing a few of the pre-production basics for any audio/visual production.

The Script

The best productions start out with a dynamite script. Take the time to put down in words what you want the audience to hear and see. A script can be as simple as a one-page general description of the words and actions laid out in one or more scenes. (The concept of "scene" applies to audio, too.) Or it can be hundreds of pages of dialog and instructions. Your script is your first and most important planning document.

Budgeting

Once you're happy with the script, work out a budget. Again, it can be as short and sweet as a single spreadsheet page. If you're renting equipment, include a line item for each piece. Labor is always the most expensive commodity; estimate the number of hours you'll need and budget for an hourly, half-day, or full-day cost for each crew member. But keep your scale in mind. You don't need to spend weeks working on a budget for a one-minute announcement by the CEO.

Location Scouting

Next, scout out the location or venue for your production. Visit the place physically, even if it's an unused office down the hall. Here are some questions to ask:

- Do I have enough physical space for cameras, microphones, tripods, etc?
- Do I have enough physical space for props, such as a desk and a chair?
- Do I have enough grounded power outlets nearby?
- Can I get access to the physical space during off hours for setup purposes?

Scheduling

When you're satisfied with the answers to the questions above, think about a detailed schedule. This is especially important for coordinating with people in leadership roles, such as corporate executives. Can the CEO show up for your recording session? Plan your production far enough ahead so you can accommodate his or her schedule. And keep in touch with his or her staff as recording or shooting approaches so you can revise your schedule if needed.

Using Contracted Labor

If you've got the budget to hire actors, take some time to learn about federal and state laws governing independent contractors. Your human resources department or your state department of labor are great places to start. It's also wise to research rules governing the use of union and non-union labor. The American Federation of Television and Radio Artists (AFTRA), the union representing many video and audio workers, has an excellent website at http://www.aftra.com/.

Connectivity

If you plan to stream something live, you will need a solid physical connection to the Internet at your shooting location. Ask the network manager how much bandwidth is available and where the network jacks are located. If all you have available is dialup, find another venue. If you have a reliable DSL/cable connection or better, you're in business. Keep in mind, however, that your actual bandwidth will vary depending on the specific type of DSL/cable connection. Ask the network manager how many kilobytes per second are going to and from your server. (We'll talk more about bandwidth in Chapter 5.) Do you need an account of some kind to connect to the local network? Be sure to have all these details in place before shooting begins.

Even if you're not planning a live broadcast, you may need to quickly upload encoded files to a server back at the office. Or you may simply need to check last-minute email. A method for connecting to your corporate network remotely could save you time and frustration.

Stay Wired for Streaming

Don't rely on a wireless connection for streaming purposes. Wireless Internet is simply too young and immature to handle the data loads and reliability needs of streaming media production. Wireless is fine, however, if you need it for more run-of-the-mill purposes, such as checking the streaming links on your organization's home page.

Be Ready for Anything

When the poet Robert Burns wrote about the failure of "the best laid plans o' mice and men" in the 18th century, he must've had a premonition about working on the Internet. In short, be ready to tackle any contingency. Good planning will see you through.

Audio and Video Inputs

Quality results require quality tools, and in this section we'll talk about the audio and video recording equipment you'll need for high-quality production. We'll also make some specific equipment recommendations, although there are many more choices than those listed here.

> ### For Best Results, Buy the Best Gear
>
> Don't skimp on equipment. You don't need to buy the most expensive state-of-the-art machinery, but you certainly want to avoid "consumer"-level equipment. Consumer cameras, tape recorders, CD players, etc., are designed to be cheap, almost throwaway. Consider your equipment an investment, not an expense.

Start with Portable Equipment

Our goal is to help you get up and running quickly, and that means selecting equipment that's easy to learn and to use. We also don't want to break your budget. To meet these goals, we'll focus on portable equipment, rather than equipment designed for studio use only. The good news is that most portable equipment can double as studio equipment in a pinch.

Digital vs. Analog Equipment

Audio and video recording devices fall into two main categories, analog and digital. Analog recording devices have been around for more than a century. The devices were first mechanical. Then electronic analog recording devices were invented in the 1920s. Analog tape recorders and cameras record light and sound as a continuously variable electrical signal, usually onto a magnetic tape wound in a plastic case, such as an audio cassette or VHS. Analog devices store a virtually infinite range of sounds and color. However, even the best analog recorders are subject to the problem of "noise"—extraneous information often introduced by the equipment itself. Noise can sometimes be filtered out during later stages of production.

Digital equipment, on the other hand, stores sound and light as binary "digits," often called "1s" and "0s." The ordered combination of these values, when interpreted by a computer, results in what we perceive as sound and light. Like analog devices, digital devices record onto magnetic tape, such as DAT for audio and DV or mini-DV for video. (See table 2.1 for a list of video formats.) Digital devices are also less susceptible to the "noise" problem. However, some audiophiles insist that analog devices record certain sounds better than digital, especially music. You may actually notice little difference in quality under 300 Kpbs. But in the long run, we think digital is a better investment.

Video Is Both Pictures and Sound

Reminder: Video tape stores both the video and audio signals. They are recorded on different areas ("tracks") on the tape. Audio tape, of course, records only audio signals.

Digital Preferred Over Analog

Since streaming relies completely on computers and computer networks, and computers only understand digital data, it makes sense to record and store sound and light digitally. Therefore, we recommend you use digital recording equipment whenever possible. However, if your budget is tight, analog equipment will work just fine, though getting the signal from the recorder to the computer may require more work, and the quality of the final output may suffer slightly.

Portable Audio Recorders and Cameras

Here are some recommendations for portable audio recorders and video cameras. These are only recommendations; you should take some time to shop around for something that meets your specific needs and budget.

Analog

Marantz PMD 222

The Marantz PMD 222 analog tape recorder is the standard portable cassette tape recorder for radio stations all over the world. It's inexpensive, rugged, and full-featured. It also has an all-important XLR microphone cable connector. (We'll talk about cables later.)

Table 2.1. Video Recording Formats

Format	Type	Quality
DigiBeta	Digital	Excellent
Betacam SP	Analog	Excellent
DV (DVCAM, Mini-DV)	Digital	Good
Digital 8	Digital	Good
S-VHS/Hi-8	Analog	Avoid
VHS	Analog	Avoid

Figure 2.1   Marantz PMD 222 analog tape recorder.

Note: You may have to buy or construct a special cable to get audio signal from the tape deck to your computer. The cable needs an RCA connector on one end and a "mini-plug" connector on the other.

Sony BVW-200

The Sony BVW-200 analog video camera with built-in recorder is a broadcast standard that records in Beta SP format. The camera uses a charged couple device (CCD), a chip that transforms light into analog electrical signals. The camera is relatively inexpensive compared to its digital counterparts.

Digital

Tascam DAP1

The Tascam DAP1 digital audio recorder is also used by broadcasters for field recording. It can record in stereo, as well as mono, and it uses digital readouts for elapsed time and other information.

Canon GL-2

The Canon GL-2 is a solid entry-level, multi-use digital video camera. It's pricier than some others, but still affordable. The camera records in mini-DV format.

Support Equipment

Good audio and video production requires dozens of moving parts, so to speak. Here's a list of items every production team needs. To save money, you can rent

Figure 2.2   Sony BVW-200 analog video recorder. The model shown was discontinued several years age. But you don't have to buy new to get the right equipment to do a good job.

Figure 2.3   Tascam DAP1 digital audio tape recorder.

Figure 2.4   Canon GL-2 digital video camera.

some of these items or buy them used. Other items you'll use primarily in the studio.

Recording Tape

Magnetic recording tape varies in quality from manufacturer to manufacturer. Use a brand name and stick with it. It's also a good idea to use 60-minute blanks. The tape itself is thicker and more durable than tape in a 90-minute or two-hour blank.

Microphones

Next to the recorder, your microphone (mic) is the most important tool in your kit. Never rely on microphones built into the recorder, whether audio recorder or camera. Internal mics or camera-mounted mics can't record decent sound worth a dang. Here are three suggestions for quality hand-held microphones:

- Electrovoice RE-50
- Shure SM-58
- Audix om7

And here are a couple of clip-on lavalier mics for video work:

- Audio Technica AT803B
- Shure MX183

Microphone Stand

The microphone stand is an often-overlooked piece of equipment. Putting your hand-held mic on a stand reduces the chance you might introduce noise when you move the mic around. It also makes it easier to point it toward a sound source, such as an actor's mouth.

Lighting Kit

It goes without saying that good video requires good lighting. A beginner's professional lighting kit starts with two lights and a carrying case. Lighting kits made by Lowel are the standard.

Headphones

Professional audio and video producers always monitor the audio via a good pair of headphones. These tell you what the microphone is picking up, allowing you to adjust placement of the microphone or the volume levels. Be sure to buy headphones whose ear cups cover the entire ear, not just part of it. That keeps out room noise. Here are suggestions for headphones:

- AKG Acoustics K141M
- Sony MDR 7506

Cables/Connectors

Cables get your information to and from devices. They should be balanced and shielded to avoid the introduction of noise from nearby electronic devices. These connectors need to be strong enough to cope with the constant banging, jiggling, and pulling they experience. Use XLR connectors whenever possible. These are the strongest available.

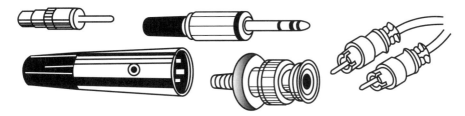

Figure 2.5 The main types of cable connectors, moving clockwise: mini (Grove), quarter-inch (Bux Communications), RCA (1 Stop Electronix), BNC (Stark Electronics), and XLR (Stark Electronics). These are the male versions. The female counterparts are usually built into the tape recorder or computer.

Walk Around Cables

Don't step on cables! There are smaller cables inside the sheathing, and stepping on them could rub off insulation, causing a short, or breaking one in two.

Audio Mixing Desks

A mixing desk is used to blend multiple recordings of audio into a single recording. For example, you can mix voice, music, and natural or ambient sound onto a single track.

These can be used for an audio-only production or for creating a highly produced audio track in a video. (By the way, you can mix audio using software. But it's not as much fun.) Two good mixing desks are the following:

- Behringer MXB 1002
- Mackie 1202 VLZ-Pro

Video Tape Recorders

You'll use a VTR (Video Tape Recorder) primarily for video tape playback, rather than recording. Like portable tape recorders and cameras, VTRs come in analog and digital flavors. Make sure you get one that's compatible with your other choices. And make sure your VTR has a FireWire/iLink connector. (More on FireWire later.) The main drawback with VTRs is cost. New ones can cost $50,000 to $100,000. But you can get used VTRs in good condition for a tenth of the price of a new one, or even less. A couple of good VTR choices are the following:

- Sony DVR-20 (analog)
- Sony DSR-11 (digital)

Note: If your camera has a FireWire connector, you can take the video/audio feed directly out of the camera and send it to your computer workstation. However, if someone else takes the video and hands you a tape, you'll need a VTR.

Compressors and Proc Amps

Compressors help you manage the volume levels in your audio. Most professional sounding audio is compressed. Here are a couple of equipment options:

- Presonius Blue Max
- FMR RNC1773

A "proc amp" (short for "processing amplifier") cleans up video signals coming out of a camera. Options include the following:

- SignVideo PA-100 (single channel)
- SignVideo PA-200 (dual channel)

Equipment Bag or Rack

Invest in a set of sturdy portable equipment cases with wheels if you have lots of equipment and need to set it up quickly. Cases also make hauling equipment on airplanes much easier.

Odds and Ends

Here are a few small, but important items to add to your shopping list:

- Duct or gaffer tape
- Connector adapters (RCA to XLR, mini to ¼ inch, etc.)
- Extra cabling
- Extra batteries and extension cords
- Small toolkit (Phillips and flathead screwdrivers, sharp knife, scissors, pliers)
- Pencil and paper
- A credit card to buy the things you forgot

Places to Buy Equipment

You can buy most, if not all, of the equipment you need online. Here are a few websites you might try:

- Broadcast Supply Worldwide (audio) http://www.bswusa.com/
- The Broadcast Store (video) http://www.bcs.tv/
- Online auction sites (Some people swear by these for mining good deals.)

Here's a tip: If you go out on location, find out where the nearest electronics store is, such as a Radio Shack. This will save you time if you discover you've forgotten a connector or you need batteries.

Get Intimate With Your Equipment

Ok, it's obvious. But just in case you didn't think of it, spend an hour getting familiar with all your new equipment. Read the manual. Plug in and unplug cables. Push buttons. Twist dials. Put in and take out tapes. As long as you're reasonably gentle, it's pretty hard to damage your new equipment. But it's a good idea to test everything.

Fundamentals of Audio Recording and Video Composition for Streams

Streaming is a new method for delivering audio and video online. That doesn't mean you need to learn brand new techniques for recording sound or composing a video shot. However, some things that work for the television screen don't work well for the computer screen. In this section, we'll review some of the fundamentals of audio and video production and offer some tips for adapting video techniques you may already know to a streaming environment.

Why Not Just Record to the Hard Disk?

We've suggested throughout this chapter that you should record your audio or video onto tape using specialized equipment, then transfer the data to your computer. But why not just record it directly onto a computer disk and save a bunch of steps? This makes sense. Several companies make specialized equipment for just this purpose, though most of it is designed for studio, not field use. And it's very expensive. For now, we suggest avoiding the temptation to record directly to your desktop personal computer or laptop. For one thing, recording on tape means you have an instant backup once you transfer all or part of your recording to your computer hard drive.

More importantly, your desktop was built for word processing and web browsing, not the intensive production of time-based audio and visual information. Your disk drive and certain other components weren't designed for the large file sizes and huge data transfer rates required for intensive audio and video production. It's true that you can perform all of the activities and procedures described in this book on a desktop computer. But if you plan to create a large number of long-form productions, i.e., longer than five minutes each, consider buying one of the professional audio or video workstations.

Audio

Sound is an incredibly rich and rewarding medium. We could spend a whole chapter just talking about the right ways to record the human voice and the thousands of animate and inanimate objects that make sounds. However, we want to put you on the right path immediately. So we're going to focus on voice, because it's the simplest type of audio for beginners, and your first audio productions are likely to be voice only. You can build on these skills if you move on to more complex types of recording, such as music.

Simple Steps for Professional Results

We're going to offer some simple steps for recording voice. You'll need some time to practice and get used to working with the equipment. But you'll get the hang of it soon enough.

First, write down what you want to say, i.e., write a script. It can be anything from hand-written notes to a professionally edited script. Write it double-spaced and in all capital letters so it'll be easy to read.

Next, find a quiet place for recording. A studio is best. But any place where interruptions are few will work. Set up your equipment so that it's all within arm's reach. And make sure you can read the volume meter, for reasons we'll explain later.

The Towel-Over-the-Head Trick

Finding a quiet place to record will be harder than you think. Once you close the door, plug in your headset and listen to what the microphone picks up. If you're in an office, you might hear the whirr of your computer's cooling fan, the whoosh of the air conditioning, or the buzz of fluorescent lights. If you have trouble finding a quiet room, try this trick. Get a light blanket or a large beach towel. Put it over your head and your microphone, as if you were in a tent. Then listen. Hopefully, the ambient sounds of your makeshift studio will be gone, or at least muted. This will lead to better sounding recordings, though you may look a bit silly to your friends and co-workers.

Check all your connections. A loose one may sound solid, but a slight jiggle could cause a momentary loss of signal. Put on your headset and plug it into your recorder. You'll hear everything coming through the microphone and going on the tape. Gather up extra cable and put it where you won't kick it or trip on it.

Put your microphone near your mouth, ideally on a microphone stand. Experiment with the distance between your mouth and the microphone for best sound. The distance is usually three to six inches. Then place the mic at a slight angle to your lips. When we say the letters "p" or "t," we tend to make extra noises with our lips and teeth. Putting the mic at an angle mitigates this problem.

Volume Levels

The most important concept in audio recording is volume level. A volume "level" is a measure of the power of the signal reaching the recording heads of the recording device. (The "head" is an electromagnet that rearranges metal oxides on the physical tape.) Too low a level means that background noise caused by electronics and other factors could overwhelm the sound you really want to hear, the voice. Too high a level could result in irritating distortion. Ever hear someone scream into a microphone? That grating sound you hear is distortion.

Monitor your levels by watching the volume meter on your tape deck. See figure 2.6 for an illustration of volume meters (sometimes called a "VU," for "volume unit," meter) you're likely to encounter.

Depending on your equipment, you need to treat the readings differently. On analog equipment, keep the needle out of the red zone as much as possible. A little bit is ok. If the needle barely nudges, your level is too low. On digital equipment, lights will be green, yellow, and red. Say a few words, and if the red lights blink a lot, your volume level is too high. If just a couple of green lights blink, the volume level is too low. If you see lots of green lights, with a smatter-

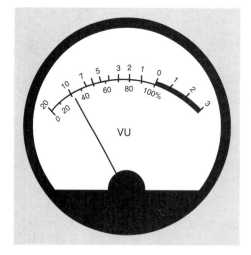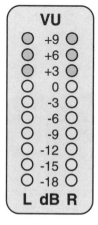

Figure 2.6 Two types of simple volume meters. The left VU meter (plugin.org.uk) is found primarily on analog equipment. The right one, often called an LED (Light Emitting Diode) peak meter (Elliott Sound Products), is usually found on digital equipment.

ing of yellow lights, your level is just right. On both digital and analog equipment, use the adjustment dial to modify your volume level up or down. Experiment and you'll find the right place. It might even be wise to turn your level down just a bit before you read your script. Some people increase their voice volume slightly when they actually start recording. By the way, if you're just learning about audio recording or plan to record only once in a while, ignore all the numbers and minus signs for now. Those are for experienced pros to figure out.

A caveat: The most expensive equipment in the world is no match for the human ear attached to a thinking brain. Use metering as a sanity check against your ears. But don't let metering overrule your own good judgment.

Volume Level vs. Volume Output

Don't confuse the volume level adjustment with the volume output into your headset. If you hear the volume in your headset go up or down, but the VU meter reading doesn't change, check whether you're turning the right dial.

Start Your Recording

If everything looks right, and you feel comfortable, push the record button (or the "play" and "record" buttons together), take a nice breath, and start reading your script. You're likely to rush through it the first time. This is a common problem for the inexperienced. Next time, slow your speaking rate by half. It'll feel odd at first. But when you play it back, it'll sound normal and easy to understand. You can also try reading while you're standing up. This lets you move at least one of your hands around, as if you were having a conversation, and this will help you sound more natural.

Read your script several times and stop recording. Rewind and listen to all the takes. If you don't like any of them, read a few more times. When you're satisfied with a take, note its location on the tape, and remove the tape from the deck. Put it in a safe place and neatly store your equipment for later use.

Video

The techniques of film and video have evolved over more than a century. When streaming video came along in the late 1990s, many producers assumed they could use the same editing techniques, shot compositions, special effects, camera movements, and other common elements of visual language. Many people were disappointed when these creative options didn't automatically translate to the streaming medium.

However, this doesn't mean you can't have a sophisticated, well-produced streaming video. Just remember that video communication over a digital network is not the same as throwing a tape into a VCR or sending a video signal over the air. Think of streaming video and other types of video as different canvases with different palettes. Once you understand your streaming palette, you can create compelling stories.

Audio and Other Rules

Before we get into the video-only material, you might review the audio section above. All the suggestions and techniques for audio-only recording apply to audio recording for video with a few variations. In addition to writing a script, for example, you should consider storyboarding your script. A storyboard is a series of drawings that help you plan each video shot. A storyboard is akin to a visual outline of your video. It's an invaluable planning and time-saving tool.

Microphones are a potential problem. You can use your audio-only microphone on a mic stand, but it's large and distracting. In the case of video, a lavalier mic is a better choice. These almost invisible devices clip on to a blouse or tie and produce a high-quality audio signal. Don't forget to check your audio levels! A great picture with bad sound is worse than a great picture with no sound.

Lighting Is Critical

Light is everything in video recording. Cameras aren't as sensitive to light as you might think. The real reason shots look good, other than good framing, is the extra light thoughtfully cast on the scene. This helps you capture all the details, the correct colors, and the correct contrast between light and shadow. You definitely need extra light indoors. And you may need it outdoors as well.

Lighting a scene for video is an art in itself. Most techniques start with the classic "three-point" system. Three lights bathe the subject in enough light for good color, contrast, and definition. Here are the elements for the three-point system:

- Key light—The key light is the main light source placed above the camera. It highlights the contours of the subject and throws deep shadows.
- Fill light—The fill light is softer than a key light, and "fills" some of the shadows. The fill light lowers the contrast between areas lit by the key light and shadows caused by the key light.
- Back light—The back light throws light behind the subject, and gives the subject a three-dimensional look by bringing it out of the background.

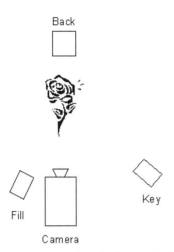

Figure 2.7 Simple three-point lighting system.

If you shoot outdoors on a day with heavy overcast, you may need to add artificial light. On a clear day, the sun provides plenty of light, but the shadows may be harsh. A simple solution is a "bounce board," a large flat panel painted white that reflects sunlight to fill in shadows.

Composition for Streaming

The video audience has grown used to productions using techniques that enrich the visual experience. Moving graphics, whip pans, fast dissolves, and soft focus have become part of our visual language. Unfortunately, most of this phraseology doesn't work with the current level of streaming technology. Why? Each time something moves in the frame, data is added to the total amount of information. To be displayed, this data has to be transmitted over the Internet. But the pipes that carry data over the Internet are still far too small to manage all the information contained in a video designed for display on a television. Therefore, we have to pare down our visual language. This doesn't mean you're limited to putting the camera on the tripod and locking it down. But it does mean you need to scale back some of your creative options and expectations.

First Warning: Know Your Audience

Good video production requires an understanding of your audience. When you produce for a streaming audience, you need to ask two additional questions: How are they connected to the Internet and what is

Continued

their connection speed? If you think your audience will watch the video primarily at dialup speeds, that is, 28.8 Kbps or 56 Kbps, you are severely limited in your visual language. The data pipes are tiny and simple visual changes from one shot to the next add enormous amounts of data. Fortunately, users are slowly migrating toward DSL/Cable connections at home. And most medium-sized businesses and large corporations have high-speed connections. This gives you more flexibility in your language choices. We'll talk more about audience analysis in Chapter 3.

Table 2.2. Typical Bandwidths and Creative Flexibility

Bandwidth	Flexibility
28.8 Kbps Dialup	Severely Limited
56 Kbps Dialup	Limited
DSL/Cable Modem	Moderate
T-1	Good
LAN	Excellent

Some Dos and Don'ts

Here are a few suggestions of techniques that translate well to streaming and those that don't. Good writing and storyboarding will help you get the most out of the techniques that work.

- Do
  - Close-ups
  - One and two shots
  - Simple patterns in clothing
  - Simple, static backgrounds
  - Simple editing, including cutaways
  - Slow camera movements
  - Large font text and graphic elements with minimal detail
- Don't Do
  - Group shots
  - High-motion, such as fast pans, wipes, or *cinema verité*
  - Quick cuts, i.e., too many shots in a brief period of time
  - Available light, unless full sunlight
  - Small text fonts or small graphic images
  - Moving graphics
  - Fast dissolves
  - Backgrounds with motion, such as rolling surf or flapping flags

Using PowerPoint in Streaming Video

Many corporate video producers are shooting speeches or demonstrations that feature Microsoft PowerPoint presentations. These are great opportunities for adding visual variety to a stream without adding tons of digital information. Here's a simple technique:

1. Record the speech and get the PowerPoint file.
2. Have a graphics person extract the slides as JPEG files. Or try the "Export to web" command in PowerPoint.
3. Using your video editing tools, drop each JPEG image into an appropriate spot in the video, keeping the audio track underneath.

Now you have a video with switches between the talking head and his or her slides. It ain't Hollywood, but it's more engaging than just the speechmaker.

A Final Word About Audio

Experienced video producers may squirm at the creative limitations presented by streaming video. You could wait 10 or 15 years for the technology to catch up to your visual storytelling skills. But businesses and consumers are demanding streaming video now. How to cope? Think about your audio. You can deliver very high quality audio even at low bandwidths. And you don't have to worry as much about the data implications of multi-track recording, sound effects, and other kinds of "ear" candy. So consider spending extra resources on a killer audio track. It might make a dull visual experience a richer multimedia experience.

A Bit of Audio and Video Theory Related to Streaming Media

We spend very little time on the theory behind digital audio and video in this book. But we thought this would be a good opportunity to give you a little bit of background before we delve into the details of the computer hardware and software.

How Digital Audio Works

Sound is complex analog vibrations in a medium, usually air, with variations in frequency, tone, and volume. These vibrations can have infinite variety, although the human ear is limited in the range of sound it can hear. Our ears convert these vibrations into analog electrical impulses. Our brain interprets and applies meaning to these impulses.

The first recording devices invented in the 19th century by Thomas Edison and others stored sound as variations in a continuous groove etched on a metal or wax cylinder or plate. To play the sound back, a motor powered by a spring or electricity turned the cylinder or plate at a constant speed. A diamond needle placed in the groove vibrated with the variations and transferred this mechanical energy to an amplifier. (Later devices used a magnet to rearrange and/or read the magnetic patterns of iron oxide crystals on Mylar tape.) The amplifier drove an electromagnet, which vibrated a rubber or paper cone. The cone's vibrations were transferred to the air, which were heard as reproduced sound.

In the digital world, an electromechanical device (the microphone) picks up sound and converts it into analog electrical impulses, much like our ears do. But when the sound goes into a computer, usually via a sound card, the specially designed semi- conductor chips take "samples" of the sound. It's as if you were at a large buffet table. You see a huge bowl of strawberries. You can't eat them all, but you can sample them and get a good idea of what the rest probably taste like.

Audio sampling is no different. You can set your sound card to take just a few samples of the incoming signal, or you can tell it to take a lot. More samples mean more information and a better representation of the sound as a whole. The number of samples you take of a signal is called the "sampling rate." The rate is expressed in hertz, a measurement of how often you take samples per second. Most samples fall in the range of 8 kilohertz ("thousands" of hertz) to 44.1 Khz.

A second factor affects the amount of information gathered by the sound card. The "bit rate" determines the amount of detail gathered from the sample, sometimes called the range of detail, resolution, or depth. Typical bit rates for digital audio include 8-bit, 16-bit, and 32-bit. (CD-quality audio is 16-bit.)

Sampling and File Size

It's worth noting here that the greater the sample frequency and larger the bit rate, the larger the file. That affects your disk storage space. Look in the section on audio and video capturing for a formula to help you determine file sizes.

How Digital Video Works

Light is waves of energy and magnetism that travel through space; the more precise term for light is "electromagnetic radiation." The waves travel at different wavelengths. Scientists measure a wavelength from the crest of one wave to the crest of the next, analogous to the waves caused by dropping a pebble into a pond. The wavelengths of light are measured in billionths of a meter. The range of electromagnetic wavelengths is enormous, but humans see only a small portion of it, known as "visible light."

Like sound, light is also measured in frequency, and the human eye perceives different frequencies as color. Color frequencies range from 430 trillion hertz (red) to 750 trillion hertz (violet). Light travels through the iris of the eye through a flexible lens, which focuses it on the retina. Cells called rods and cones transform the light waves into electrical impulses that travel along the optic nerve to the brain. The 120 million rods in the average eye pick up dim light and motion. The six million or so cones specialize in color reception.

The first artificial light-gathering and storage device appeared in 1826, when a French inventor named Joseph Nicéphore Niépce made a picture of the roofs of some houses in his neighborhood. He gathered light using an old device called a *camera obscura* and stored the image on a pewter plate coated with a chemical akin to asphalt. Photography advanced to the point in 1895 when fellow Frenchman Louis Lumiere invented a camera that could take photographs quickly, one after the other, on a long roll of cellophane film. (Lumiere's invention could also process and project the film.) Lumiere himself predicted the movie industry would never amount to anything.

With the invention of radio a few years later, inventors began to think of ways to send moving images electromagnetically. One technique that gained favor was developed in the 1920s by Philo T. Farnsworth. He found a way to scan the surface of a light-gathering device (called a "pickup") and transform the signal into electrical impulses. Think of how you read a page in this book. You start at the top left, go across the page, start again at the next line, and repeat the process to the end of the page. A camera does this work at nearly the speed of light. A television reverses this process. You see an image because the scan happens so quickly. It's the same principle, known as "persistence of vision," that makes the millions of images on film appear as one moving image. To store analog images, video engineers took the cue from audio engineers and created large versions of audio tape recorders to record visual and audio signals.

Farnsworth's analog methods dominated video technology until the 1980s and the advent of the digital camera. A digital video camera measures light in tiny pieces called "pixels," assigns a value to each, and converts the value into "1s" and "0s." Like digital audio, digital video samples the video signal at a given rate and a given depth in bits.

However, digital cameras gather far more information than we can store efficiently. Therefore, electronics in the camera or elsewhere "compress" or remove some of the redundant information. (We'll speak more of compression in Chapter 3.) To display the video information, the computer reverses the compression, or "decompresses" the signal stored in the digital video signal or file, and illuminates individual pixels on the monitor, somewhat like the drops that create an image in a Jackson Pollock painting.

Digital Video vs. Digital Movies

Some people make a distinction between digital video and digital movies. We can think of digital video as video meant for display exclusively on a computer screen. Digital video comes in a variety of formats, plays off hard drives or CD-ROM drives, and includes streaming media.

Digital movies, on the other hand, generally refer to movies stored on Digital Video Disc (DVD). DVD movies follow a common format, and require special hardware. A DVD movie can also be played at full screen with very high quality, unlike its digital video cousin.

Is Digital Really Better?

Many people still debate the relative advantages of digital recording over analog recording, despite the ascendance and dominance of digital. Here's a list to help you make up your own mind.

Advantages

- More precise recording than analog
- Copies are exact, without data loss when copies are made from copies
- Easier to edit and manipulate
- Cheaper to design and build digital recording and editing equipment

Disadvantages

- Exact copies make piracy, that is, theft easier. (With analog, copies of copies look worse than the original.)
- Digital video files are large and awkward to work with.
- Some audiophiles believe digital recordings lack a certain warmth and smoothness.

Common Source File Formats

You'll come across a variety of file formats as you work with computer audio and video. "Source" file formats, as far as this book is concerned, are formats used to store audio and video in a computer before they are transformed or "encoded" into streamable formats. (A format is simply a way to organize data in a storage medium.) To keep things simple, we like to think of these formats as "raw", just like the raw ingredients of a good pizza, before they are "cooked" into a format specifically designed for Internet delivery.

Table 2.3. Common source data file formats you'll encounter in the world of digital audio and video. You'll transform files in these formats to streaming media formats

Name	Type	Extension
AIFF	Audio	`.aif, .aiff`
AU	Audio	`.au`
MIDI	Audio	`.mid, .midi`
MOD	Audio	`.mod`
VOC	Audio	`.voc`
WAV	Audio	`.wav`
AVI	Video	`.avi`
MOV	Video	`.mov`
MPEG	Video	`.mpg, .mpeg`

Your Dream Workstation

Now that you've purchased or rented your audio and/or video equipment, it's time to talk about building an editing workstation. You can spend tens of thousands of dollars on non-linear editing hardware and software packages. You can also spend a lot less by building your own using off-the-shelf parts and packaged software. You'll need to pay particular attention to some of the parts, notably the hard drive. But if you don't mind tinkering with computers, you can build a darn good workstation at no more than half the cost of a package deal. Note that your editing workstation doubles as a streaming media encoding workstation, though you can separate the two functions on two different computers.

The following are the main points of difference between the hardware of a standard desktop computer you buy at a retail store and an editing workstation:

- Processing power
- Memory (RAM)
- Storage (Hard disk)

Rule of thumb for all these: More is better. So buy or assemble the most powerful equipment you can manage. See Table 2.4 for some requirements and recommendations.

Going Non-Linear When Editing

"Non-linear" editing refers to the ability to move elements of video and audio around via an editing software package. It's very similar to cutting and pasting words, sentences, or paragraphs on a word processor. Before computers, most editing happened in a linear fashion, that is, physical film clips or tape clips were assembled one after the other.

Table 2.4. Minimum and recommended personal computer* hardware and software requirements for a do-it-yourself, non-linear editing and encoding workstation

Minimum Requirements	500 Mhz Pentium II
	96MB of RAM
	500 MB disk storage
	16-bit sound card and speakers
	16-bit color video display
	Microsoft Windows 98SE/XP
Recommended Requirements	800+ Pentium III processor
	256 MB of RAM
	1 GB disk storage
	16-bit sound card and speakers
	24-bit color video display
	Windows XP Pro

*Minimum hardware for Apple users is the PowerMac G3, with the PowerMac G5 recommended.

The hard drive recommendations in Table 2.4 are actually pretty dinky. They'll get you started, but you're better off getting the biggest hard drive you can afford. And try to get a SCSI (pronounced "scuzzy") hard drive, not the standard IDE hard drive. SCSI drives are more expensive, but they perform better under the demanding conditions of audio and video editing.

Fired Up About FireWire

One of the best hardware developments in recent years is FireWire, which was developed by Apple Computer as an ultra-fast method of getting large amounts of data from one device to another. Also called i.Link or IEEE 1394 after the standards body that adopted it, FireWire is ideal for moving video and audio data from a digital recording device such as a DV camera to an editing and encoding workstation. You can move 400 MBs of data a second over a FireWire cable up to 4.5 meters long. How does this apply to you? Make sure any video cards you install have FireWire capability.

Audio and Video Cards

Analog signals from analog audio recorders and cameras have to be converted to binary 1s and 0s before a computer can manipulate them. Specialized hardware in the form of a "capture card" does this work. You'll need to install one or more of these cards before you can work with your audio or video.

> ## Audio Card/Sound Card
>
> Most off-the-shelf personal computers include a sound card, which can double as an audio capture card. These are enough to get you going. But if you plan a large audio project, upgrade to a professional-level audio card.

Suggested Audio and Video Card Options

- Audio Cards
  - Minimum: Factory-installed sound card
  - Recommended: Creative Labs Sound Blaster Audigy MP3
- Video Cards
  - Minimum: ViewCast Osprey 210 (Audio and video combined)
  - Recommended: ViewCast Osprey 500 DV

Editing Software

Editing software lets you manipulate your audio and video files in ways unimaginable a generation ago. You can cut and paste portions of audio or video from the same file or different files. You can have an almost unlimited number of tracks. You can filter out certain kinds of audio-destroying noise or add video effects, such as fades. You'll find yourself spending hours just playing with these software packages. Here are a few choices:

- Audio Editing
  - Syntrillium CoolEdit 2000
  - Sonic Foundry Sound Forge
- Video Editing
  - Sonic Foundry Vegas
  - Adobe Premiere

A Studio Environment

It's true you can produce audio and video on your desktop computer in your office. But a quiet, well-organized work environment devoted to audio and video editing is best. Think about converting an unused office into an editing booth. Put sound baffles on the walls and weather stripping around the door. Organize your equipment so that everything is in reach, cables and other

Figure 2.8   Screenshot of CoolEdit 2000.

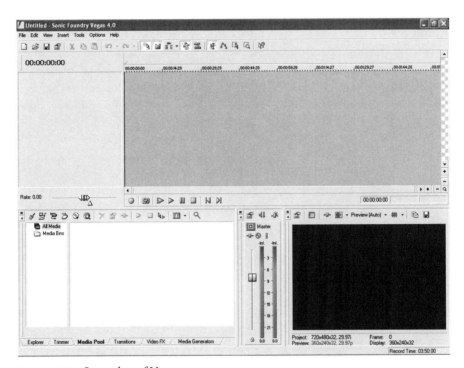

Figure 2.9   Screenshot of Vegas.

equipment are properly stored, and you have a good chair. You'll probably spend a lot of time in here, so you might as well be comfortable!

Moving Your Audio and Video From Recording Device to Workstation

One of the most critical tasks you'll undertake as a streaming media specialist is "capturing." This is the process of moving data from your audio or video recording device to your computer workstation. It's important to do this well, because after you've captured the data, it's much harder to fix problems that may have been introduced by poor capturing technique.

Much of the capture procedure is driven by the particular hardware and software you use. Read the instruction manual for both the audio and/or video capture hardware, particularly if you are unfamiliar with FireWire. Hardware manufacturers often bundle simple editing software packages with their cards. These give you a chance to experiment with the hardware, though the software is rarely up to professional production standards. If you have purchased editing software, be patient while you learn the software's intricacies. Fortunately, most editing software uses familiar concepts such as Play/Pause/Stop and Record for basic tasks.

You may want to optimize your workstation before capturing, especially if you've been doing some other intensive work. Here's a checklist:

- Defragment your hard drive.
- Turn off network access and file sharing.
- Close all other programs, especially those that access your hard drive.
- Monitor your system resources to make sure the computer has enough power to keep up with the work it has to do.

Prepare to Capture

Get yourself organized at your workstation with all your recording equipment. Hook everything up and make sure you can monitor output from your recorder via your computer. That way, you'll hear/see the same thing that's going on the hard drive.

Disk Space Needs

You'll be stunned how fast your hard disk fills up when you start capturing video, especially if you use uncompressed video. To avoid the dreaded "disk full" error, here's a quick formula for calculating how much disk space you need for a given clip:

$$(\text{pixel width}) \times (\text{pixel height}) \times (\text{color bit depth}) \times (\text{fps})$$
$$\times (\text{duration in seconds})/8,000,000$$

For example, here's a potential calculation for a 2-minute clip:

$$320 \times 240 \times 24 \times 30 \times 120 / 8{,}000{,}000 = 829.44 \text{ megabytes}$$

Be aware that some Microsoft Windows and Apple Macintosh file systems limit individual file sizes to 2 gigabytes (2048 megabytes). That means if you have a long production, you have to either reduce certain parameters, such as color depth, or use editing software that can support file sizes greater than 2 GB. If you have a very long video, you may be able to glue individual pieces together after encoding with utilities provided by the encoding software vendor, such as RealNetworks or Microsoft.

Time to Capture

Let's assume you have some tapes in front of you. Find the specific sections you want to capture. Don't capture the whole thing; that wastes time and disk space. Now choose some capture settings. This is critical! If you don't capture at the right settings, you could have trouble later when you encode. You may have to experiment some, but here are some basic audio capture settings:

- Bit depth: 16-bit
- Sample rate: 44.1 kilohertz
- Format: WAV (`.wav`)

And here are some basic video capture settings:

- Frame size: 320 × 240
- Frame rate: 30 fps (frames per second)
- Compression ratio: Lowest available

Video capturing includes a few other parameters to consider. Microsoft suggests that if you use a video monitor, adjust the SMPTE color bars (a standard color gauge in television and video production) and then adjust your computer monitor to match using a high-resolution computer bitmap of the SMPTE bars. Then adjust your video capture levels (hue, saturation, and brightness) so that the picture matches the video monitor. Microsoft also suggests you may also want to capture the YUY2 (4:2:2) pixel format for optimal use of its technology.

FireWire and Frame Settings

If you use FireWire, you don't need to worry about setting frame sizes, frames per second, etc. The technology automatically transfers the digital video data at full-frame size and 30 fps using the built-in digital video compression.

You should also set audio levels in the editing software. These usually take the form of peak level meters. (See the earlier section on volume levels.)

Now that you're ready to capture, click Record, and the hardware converts the analog signal from the recording device to the 1s and 0s computers understand. The software applies its settings and stores the data on your hard drive. In a few moments, you'll have your source audio or video file, all ready for encoding.

Please Respect Copyrights

Copyright, that is, the rights of authors to enjoy the financial benefits of their work by controlling who may copy it, is one of the hottest Internet issues today. One need only mention words like "Napster" and "piracy" to start an argument. You may have your own views on the issue. The law says authors or their agents are the only ones who can grant you the right to copy and distribute their work. Before you capture audio or video and create a streaming version, please ask the copyright owner whether you can do so. Let's not give the lawyers any more work than they already have.

Chapter Summary

In this chapter, you learned about planning a streaming media production. We looked at various kinds of recording equipment and made some recommendations. We talked about the differences between analog recording and digital recording. We offered some techniques for recording audio and video that will lead to good streaming media results. We detailed requirements for a starter editing and encoding workstation, including the all-important audio and video capture cards. And we gave you an idea of how the capturing process works. Next, we'll take your captured audio or video and create an encoded file.

Streaming Media Timeline

The following timeline shows many of the milestones in the development of streaming media technology and the streaming media industry.

1992
- Multicast Backbone (MBone) deployed
- Real Time Transport Protocol (RTP) version 1
- Audiocast of 23rd Internet Engineering Task Force (IETF) meeting

Continued

1994
- Rolling Stones concert on MBone

1995
- Progressive Networks' RealAudio launched
- Xing Technologies launches MPEG tool suite
- KPIG-FM in Santa Cruz, Calif., is the first live Internet radio station

1996
- Vivo Software launches VivoActive
- VXtreme launches Web Theater
- Microsoft launches Netshow
- Macromedia launches Flash 1.0
- Real Time Streaming Protocol (RTSP) submitted to IETF

1997
- Microsoft buys VXtreme
- Progressive Networks changes name to RealNetworks
- RealVideo launched

1998
- RealNetworks buys Vivo Software
- MPEG-4 standard finalized
- Apple Computer announces QuickTime Streaming
- RealSystem G2 (6.0) introduced

1999
- RealNetworks buys Xing Technologies
- Netshow becomes Windows Media

2000
- RealPlayer reaches 100 million users
- Windows Media 7.0 released

2001
- RealNetworks launches paid media subscription service
- RealNetworks lays off 20% of its workforce
- Microsoft investigated by European Union for alleged anti-trust violations related to streaming media players

2002
- RealSystem Mobile announced
- RealNetworks reports 750,000 paid subscribers
- Windows Media Series 9 released
- Macromedia Flash MX released

2003

- Microsoft announces Windows Media support in Windows Mobile operating system
- RealNetworks buys Listen.com and Rhapsody music service

2004

- RealNetworks announces RealPlayer 10
- Microsoft announces screenings of five full-length feature films from the Sundance Film Festival using Windows Media 9

This timeline is based on a 2002 presentation by Eckehard Steinbach of the Technical University of Munich, Germany.

3 Prepare Your Audio and Video

Terms to Know

Optimize: Streaming media producers optimize audio and video files before encoding by applying various filters or cropping techniques to remove unwanted audio noise or video artifacts.

Codec: A codec is a computer algorithm that removes certain amounts and types of data from the source audio or video file. The resulting file is much smaller than the source file, though it retains most of the audio and visual quality.

Bit rate: In the context of a streaming media file, the bit rate refers to the amount of data transferred across the Internet from the file per second. This should not be confused with the "bit rate" of captured audio and video files, which refers to the amount of detail gathered during the capturing process.

Plug-in (with respect to media players): A streaming media plug-in is software that works within a web browser to play streaming media files within the browser window, as opposed to a stand-alone media player window.

Coming into the Home Stretch

You've survived the initial shock of your boss's request to produce a new video for the Las Vegas Hardware Hype and Vaporware Show. And after carefully studying Chapter 2, you gathered the equipment, shot some video, and captured it to disk. You feel pretty good about the results. But the deadline is coming up fast, and you need to put some time into the project at home over the weekend.

Can you work on streaming media at home? You bet. Streaming media is simple enough that even home computers can perform most of the basic production tasks. This is particularly true with audio, since most home computers come with a sound card already installed and basic editing software. Video is more demanding. But if you're a computer hobbyist comfortable with adding new cards to your PC and learning new software, streaming video is within your reach.

Let's imagine you have rendered a video at work and now you need to encode it over the weekend. You've burned the video to a CD and taken it home. Your home machine meets the hardware and software requirements for capturing and encoding discussed in Chapter 2. (See Table 2.4. By the way, you don't need a video capture card if all you're doing is encoding.) You've downloaded and installed one or more of the free encoders. (See the section on encoders in Chapter 1.) If you're lucky, your boss says it's okay to install your editing software on your home computer. (We can dream, can't we?)

You're almost ready. First, we need to discuss media players in a bit more detail. We'll also help you choose the right streaming media format for your audience. Then we'll talk about ways to optimize your audio and/or video before encoding, so that you get the most out of the encoder's features. Finally, we'll show you encoding step-by-step. By the time Monday rolls around, you'll be ahead of the game.

Home users and hobbyists: This chapter starts to get really technical, but as you read in the introductory paragraphs above, you don't have to be a genius or own the latest and greatest computer equipment to create streaming media files. You can, if you like, ignore most of the technical mumbo-jumbo and get right to the procedures. But then it's always better to understand something about what you're doing. Agree?

Streaming Media Players

One of the decisions you'll make as a streaming media producer is "platform," that is, which one or more of the several streaming media technologies you'll favor for your project. You'll have to decide whether to use systems designed by RealNetworks, Microsoft, Apple Computer, Macromedia, an open standard such as MPEG, or some combination. Your decision will be driven in part by the installed base of players on the computers of your expected audience.

What Is a "Media Player?"

A "media player" in the streaming context is software that receives audio and video data sent by a streaming server or a web server. The data comes from an audio or video file specially modified (encoded) for continuous transmission over the Internet. During transmission, the media player is in constant contact with the server to ensure delivery of all the data. The media player converts the data into information that can be displayed on a screen or drive speakers to create sound.

Hmm. That's not totally accurate. If we were marketing experts (which we're not), we'd define a media player this way: A media player is an opportunity to capture the attention of an Internet user with a compelling audio and visual experience in order to impress the user with a particular brand and/or convert the user into a paying customer.

Actually, both descriptions are accurate. The point is that the major proprietary streaming media players double as media playback applications and opportunities to market goods and services. If you want to understand streaming media, you should understand that one doesn't usually exist without the other in some form. That's why media players offer so much more than Play/Pause/Stop.

Software manufacturers sell their products primarily on the strength of the software's features. If you carefully examine all the features of the leading streaming media players, you'll find incredible similarity. They may look different, the commands and menus have different names and layouts, and the underlying code may be different, but the number and types of features related to audio and video streaming are remarkably similar. This is especially true for the two heavyweights, RealNetworks and Microsoft. They are like two evenly matched boxers. Each punch and counterpunch keeps the score even. At this point, we recommend you defer questions about which platform to use until you understand the audience you want to reach. That's discussed in the next section.

How Media Players Make Money

You may ask, if the media players are so similar, how do the software companies make money with their media players? We'll discuss basic business models in Chapter 5, but the short answer is "content." Ultimately, the user wants to hear or watch interesting things with his or her media player. The number and type of doohickeys and whatsits in the software are largely irrelevant in the long run. The streaming company that can deliver the most compelling content wins.

Choosing the Right Streaming Format: Evaluating Your Audience and Resources

Now comes one of your most difficult decisions. Which format(s) should I choose that will serve my audience's needs? You'll struggle over this one. It might even keep you awake at night. The best way to cope is research, research, research. Understand and analyze your audience and the resources you have at hand as thoroughly as possible. That will lead to a good decision.

Professional media producers always start with the audience. Who is the man, woman, or child we want to reach? What are their characteristics? Are we aiming at a mass audience or a niche audience? What makes our target audience different from the general audience? Once the audience is identified, the message is tailored to resonate as strongly as possible with the target.

Streaming media producers also start with audience. But they have to ask some very specific questions related primarily to the audience's capability to hear or view the content they produce. Put another way, television producers don't have to worry whether the family TV can show the Video of the Week. That's because television technology is just about the same everywhere. But the capabilities of office or home computers and their Internet connections differ wildly. Streaming producers have to take these variations into account.

Here are some variables to evaluate as you decide which streaming media platform(s) work best for your situation.

External vs. Internal

You can roughly divide the entire universe of streaming media users into people external to your organization or internal to your organization. You have virtually no control over the types of hardware, software, or Internet connections of external users. These users could include Joe Sixpack at his desktop computer surfing the Net for entertainment or information. External users can also be a very specific group of people, such as Joe Sixpack Who Drinks Triple Caffeine Sugar Juice. Whether it's a mass audience or a niche audience, you'll have to keep in mind a wide variety of computer configurations and Internet connection types.

You have much more control over an audience internal to your network, at least in theory. Most large organizations try to limit the configurations of desktop and laptop computers for ease of maintenance. Joe Sixpack's office computer is likely to be very similar to Jane Executive's desktop in the same company. And connectivity within an organization is likely to be similar across the network.

Server   **Internet**   **Client**

Figure 3.1   You have no control over your network delivery conditions once the data enters the Internet "cloud."

Internet vs. Intranet

The Internet has been described as a vast, undifferentiated cloud between the starting place of data and the destination. This means you have zero control over the network conditions at any given moment of your streaming media broadcast to an external audience. Some people have used the term "net weather" to describe the capricious nature of Internet conditions. One minute you may have summer sunshine, the next, a winter blizzard. You simply have to accept this fact when streaming to large numbers of external users. You can take some comfort in the fact that streaming media systems are designed to cope with unpredictable conditions.

You have more control over conditions on an intranet, much like you have control over the heat and air conditioning in your house. Network administrators set the rules and parameters for network conditions on an intranet. This is especially true for single buildings or corporate campuses.

Operating Systems and the Media Player

Consumers and corporations have only two choices for desktop/laptop operating system environments: Microsoft Windows and Apple Computer's operating systems. (Some say desktops and laptops running on the Linux operating system may gain traction in the next few years. But it's too soon to tell.)

Microsoft overwhelms Apple in terms of deployment in the marketplace. It likes to tout this dominance as "creating a standard platform for personal computing." But it ain't that simple. There have been six major versions of Windows: Windows 3.1, Windows 95, Windows 98, Windows ME, Windows 2000, and Windows XP. All are still in use somewhere, though newer versions tend to replace older versions over time. Microsoft engineers are coding more versions of Windows all the time. Apple also has several versions of its operating system still in use. Its latest product, OS X, is a radical departure from previous Apple OSs, in that the new version is based on completely different code.

These "upgrades" over the past 10 years or so create enormous headaches for the streaming media producers, especially those who want to reach a large external audience. You don't have to worry so much about the operating system itself. But you do have to worry about the media players that work on that system.

Here's an example: Windows Media Player 6.4 was "bundled," that is, included, with Windows 98. But the streaming video quality of those days was poor, compared to today's video quality. However, if you think you need to create video for those players, you may have to settle for inferior video quality, potentially alienating users with later versions of Windows and Windows Media Player. If you decide to cater to later versions of Windows/Windows Media Player, you may alienate users of Windows Media Player 6.4 by forcing them to upgrade, raising the "hassle factor." (See below.)

The problem is worse with RealPlayer, QuickTime Player, and Flash. RealPlayer is bundled with Microsoft Windows by some computer manufacturers, and not by others. RealNetworks has developed at least six versions of its player since 1995. (We've lost count.) QuickTime Players are on virtually every recent Apple machine, but comparatively few Windows machines. Almost every web browser has the Flash plug-in, but it has gone through at least eight versions since 1.0 in 1996.

Before you down another dose of your ulcer medication, consider your audience. Let's say you want to reach a niche audience of graphic artists and web designers. Most of these professionals prefer the Apple platform. Perhaps you can safely choose QuickTime streams, because it's almost certain your audience has the QuickTime player on their computers. Here's the lesson: Carefully analyze your audience for clues that can help you reduce the chance that your streams are incompatible with an individual audience member's operating system and media player.

The Hassle Factor

We've mentioned the frustrating lack of knowledge and control you have regarding the operating systems and accompanying media players on the computers of an external audience. A related problem is lack of knowledge or control when it comes to specific pieces of software that may not have been shipped with a media player you're targeting. That can lead to player behavior that can confuse and alienate a user.

Let's say you've decided your audience has a certain version of a media player. You've encoded your file to match your knowledge of that player, based on your own testing. However, for one reason or another, a number of players out in the world don't have a key component installed by default. When the user tries to play your stream, a message appears that suggests he or she download a component or upgrade the player completely. The message may intimidate the user, and he or she may stop the playback attempt. Or the user may be sophisticated enough to brush off the message, take the time to download and install the component or upgrade, and continue the session. Your analysis of your audience should give you some idea of how well an individual audience member is likely to tolerate this hassle.

Again, producers targeting an internal audience have it easier. It's very likely that your information technology department limits the time and method of component upgrades or new software installations. This means you don't have to worry as much about confusing messages related to media player capabilities.

Early Adopters vs. Late Adopters

Various technology observers divide people who adopt new technologies into four groups: Innovators, Early Adopters, the Early Majority, and Laggards (See Figure 3.2). These categories can help you choose streaming formats that cater to your audience's attitude toward the online experience.

For example, you may determine that your audience is made up of gaming crazy, extreme sporting uber-geeks who think last week's product is so last week. Chances are they have the latest streaming media player running on the newest version of Windows or OS X. They probably have high-speed connectivity at home. You could take the risk of using the latest streaming codecs and high-bandwidth delivery. Using codecs from 1996 would definitely turn off this audience, dude (or dudette, as the case may be).

High Bandwidth vs. Low Bandwidth

The amount of bandwidth available to you and your audience may be the single most important factor determining your decision about platform and content. The more bandwidth on your side and the end user's side, the more likely you can satisfy your audience's expectation for a radio- or television-like streaming experience. This is especially important if you want to reach an external Internet audience.

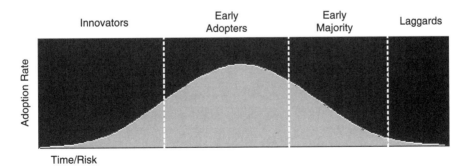

Figure 3.2 The technology adoption curve. The rate of adoption rises with time, then falls as the population likely to risk the technology falls. Innovators try everything new just because it's new. Early Adopters see the competitive advantage of a new technology and try it out, even if it's not mature. The Early Majority follows the crowd. Laggards, whom we like to call "Kickers & Screamers," would rather swallow molten lead than try any new technology.

The trends are in your favor. According to Arbitron's 2003 *Internet and Multimedia 11* report, 21 percent of all Americans have broadband cable or digital subscriber line (DSL) access at home. That's up from 7 percent in 2001. Streaming media usage and adoption tends to follow the broadband deployment trends.

Of course, the flip side is that 80 percent or so of external users access the Internet via a dialup connection, most likely at 56 kilobytes per second. The audio experience for this audience is acceptable. But the video experience is terrible. If you decide your target audience is primarily on dialup, your audio options are decent. But your video options are extremely limited.

If you're focused on an audience within the boundaries of a corporate network, you have more options. Many small organizations with 10-megabit Ethernet networks have more bandwidth than they can use, and you could take advantage of that extra capacity with streaming. You may face a different limitation: the number of people you can serve at one time. For example, if you have a 10-megabit local area network (LAN), and your boss will only accept high-quality video streams taking up 250 kilobytes per second each, you're limited to 40 simultaneous users. (It's really closer to 20; 40 simultaneous 250K streams would essentially freeze the entire network.)

Organizational Relationships

Each and every organization depends on relationships with other organizations to thrive. An educational institution may depend on a particular set of major enterprise-funded foundations for annual support. A single individual donor may be the lifeblood of a community not-for-profit. The lion's share of a small business's revenue may come from a single customer. If your target audience includes people who form a key business relationship, it makes sense to check that group's streaming capabilities. If you choose Microsoft technology, and you later find out your key customer or client prefers RealNetworks' technology, you could be in deep trouble.

Organizational Capabilities

Your organization may have capabilities you don't know about. For example, you may already have Windows Media Services set up on your network. Or your account with your Internet service provider may include RealServer. Talk to your web developer. He or she may be familiar with QuickTime, but not RealNetworks or Microsoft streaming media systems. These existing capabilities will have a major influence on your choice of streaming format, even if your audience analysis goes contrary to your analysis of internal resources.

Audience Evaluation Scenarios

External Audience

You volunteer for a youth sports association in a community with a high percentage of technology workers. The sports association has received a generous technology grant from a locally based Fortune 1000 company that competes with Microsoft. The association's board has accepted your proposal to record its annual awards ceremony for archiving on the Internet. About half the town's residents have broadband connections at home. You decide that the most likely viewers are parents and friends of team members, and your informal telephone survey of parents shows they prefer RealPlayer. How do you use this knowledge to design your streaming?

- Platform: RealNetworks RealPlayer/Helix
- Media Player Version: RealPlayer 7 (This is about three years old. Newer versions will be able to play streams designed for RealPlayer 7.)
- Streams: One audio stream for dialup users. One 225K video stream for broadband users.

Internal Audience

You work for a health care company that depends on video training. About 1,000 employees work in several small buildings connected with a high-speed LAN. Most of the employees are comfortable with computers, but they are not technology workers per se. A few workers sometimes have trouble understanding things beyond simple printing or email. Your chief financial officer spent 10 years at Microsoft before starting at your company last year, and he's okayed spending for a desktop/laptop operating system upgrade to Windows XP. The upgrade project manager and the human resources director like your idea of providing video training online. How do you use this knowledge to design your streaming project?

- Platform: Microsoft Windows Media Server
- Media Player Version: Windows Media Player 8 (bundled with Windows XP)
- Streams: One 225K video stream, limited to three simultaneous connections.

Table 3.1. Audience Bandwidth Targets. When you encode audio or video, you will encode a bit rate slightly lower than the maximum bit rate available in a given connection. That's because networked computers need some "headroom" for transmitting certain kinds of network control information. You should also note that the bit rate can vary from moment to moment, but over time the rate will be about the number you choose

Target Bandwidth	Maximum Bit Rate
28.8 Kbps dialup	20 Kbps
56 Kbps dialup	34 Kbps
Corporate LAN (intranet)	150 Kbps
256 Kbps cable/DSL	225 Kbps
384 Kbps cable/DSL	350 Kbps
512 Kbps cable/DSL	450 Kbps

Making a Decision

You've done a careful analysis of your audience and your resources. But you're still having trouble deciding which streaming platform and format will work best for you. We've put together a decision matrix that might help. A decision matrix lists all the important criteria and weighs them according to their importance. Then you give each platform a rating. Multiply the rating by the weight for a score. Add up the scores, and see which platform wins. A warning: Don't let the decision matrix make your decision for you. It's just a way to quantify intangibles. Ultimately, you have to make the final judgment based on your knowledge and experience.

Product Reviews: Useful or Not?

One way to evaluate a streaming media platform is by reading product reviews. Many consumer and industry magazines review each new release of streaming media software using internally developed benchmarks. They develop their own hardware configurations and they hire independent consultants. For example, *Network Computing* gave Apple Computer and RealNetworks grades of "B+" in a 2002 comparison. Microsoft got a "C–." (Macromedia wasn't reviewed.) On the other hand, an independent study by the University of Ferrara in Italy rated RealNetworks, Microsoft, and Apple Computer 1, 2, and 3, respectively, in a quality test of mobile streaming systems. (Again, Macromedia wasn't reviewed.)

Box continues on page 99

Table 3.2. A Streaming Media Platform and Format Decision Matrix

Streaming Media Platforms and Formats

Audience Criteria	Weight	RealNetworks		Microsoft		Apple		Macromedia	
		Rating	Score	Rating	Score	Rating	Score	Rating	Score
External									
Internal									
Internet									
Intranet									
Operating Sys.									
Media Player									
Low Bandwidth									
High Bandwidth									
Innovator									
Early Adopter									
Early Majority									
Laggard									
Hassle Factor									
Relationships									
Resources									
Totals									

Here are instructions for using this decision matrix:

1. Give each audience criterion a weight from 1 (not important) to 10 (very important).
2. Rate how well each platform meets the criterion.
3. Multiply the weight by the rating for a score.
4. Add the score for each platform. The highest score best meets the audience criteria.

Product Reviews: Useful or Not?—cont'd

Product reviews resemble movie reviews. When a vendor gets a good review, a hyperventilating press release follows within 10 seconds on a slow day. About the only thing missing is the full-page newspaper ads that scream "Brilliant!" or "Ground breaking!" or "Cool!" If a vendor gets a bad review, it may cry "Foul!" and try to discredit the tester's criteria or methodology. So then, reviews may not help much after all.

Optimize Your Audio

We talked in Chapter 2 about the importance of good audio-capturing technique as a critical step toward creating streaming audio that sounds great. You should probably spend a few minutes going over those techniques. Remind yourself about the importance of volume levels. The techniques are particularly vital for encoded audio you may broadcast via dialup connections, which have a narrower margin of error.

However, even the most experienced streaming pros find problems with audio after it's been captured. For example, you may not have noticed the quiet buzz caused by an overhead fluorescent lamp. The whoosh of the air conditioning may be particularly loud. Or the presenter uses a few too many "aahs" and "umms." You can fix these problems in the editing software. Furthermore, the software can be used to manipulate the entire audio file to make the final encoded product sound even better.

We've found it's best to perform these tasks in a certain order. Here's a quick checklist:

- ✓ Editing
- ✓ Equalization
- ✓ Compression
- ✓ Normalization
- ✓ DC Offset
- ✓ Noise Reduction

Editing

The art of public speaking has gone the way of the horse and buggy. You could argue that the advent of recorded speech meant the end of public speaking.

That's because recordings can be manipulated to make a speaker sound better. This is an extreme view; witness the brilliant oratory skills of many clergymen and women.

Most people, of course, don't have these skills. Audio editing tools exist to compensate for the problems caused by long pauses, backtracking, coughs, cleared throats, and other distracting mistakes or extraneous sounds made by public speakers. Experiment with your editing software to remove these elements, not just to make the speaker sound better, but to make the audio more "listenable." It's hard to listen to a presentation constantly interrupted by "aahs" and "umms." Don't forget that when you remove these things, you should listen to the change and fiddle with it if it sounds odd. Don't be afraid! Software editors are "non destructive." You can always Undo.

Equalization

Sometimes you may find, despite your best efforts at recording and capturing, the file just doesn't sound "right." Trust these instincts and be fearless about manipulating the way the audio sounds to your ears. You may discover, for example, that the speaker sounds "muddy," that is, there's a lot of lower frequency sound, but not a lot of higher frequency sound to give each word definition. One way to solve this problem is "equalization" or "eq'ing." Equalization is the process of turning up ("boosting") or turning down ("attenuating") small frequency ranges within audio. In the case of a muddy-sounding voice, you can try turning up the higher frequencies and turning down the low frequencies. Try attenuating frequencies below 100 Hz and boosting frequencies in the 1 to 4 kHz range.

You may already have some equalization skills. Most home stereos and many car stereos have simple built-in graphic equalizers. These are the gizmos with "slide faders" that move up and down, changing parts of the audio. A popular eq setting these days is a huge boost in bass response, which results in that "BOOM BOOM" sound favored by certain male juveniles. (Large bass speakers help.)

Your audio editing software should have a graphic equalizer, along with some presets. Again, don't hesitate to play with the settings and learn what works best. But work with moderation. You'll find that small adjustments go a long way.

Dynamic Range and Compression

One of the most important optimizations you perform on audio files is "compression." Don't confuse this with encoding, which is sometimes called "compression." Encoding removes data from a file to make it smaller and

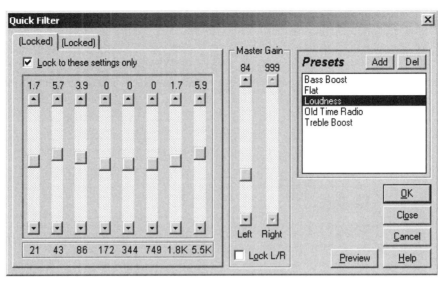

Figure 3.3 A typical software graphic equalizer (CoolEdit).

The Difference Between Voice and Music

It's important that you understand the basic difference between voice and music from an audio engineering standpoint. Audio pros talk about the difference in terms of "dynamic range," which can be though of as the span of volume from quiet to loud of all the sounds in a particular file. Music, typically, has a wide dynamic range. Think of Tchaikovsky's *1812 Overture*. In the space of a few seconds, the music can go from the quiet of a few wind instruments to cannon fire. The music has a wide dynamic range.

Voice normally has a narrow dynamic range. The next time you have a lengthy conversation with your best friend, listen for the range of quiet places to loud places. Unless your friend likes to yell a lot, the dynamic range will be fairly narrow. Have you ever noticed how terrible music sounds over the telephone, while your best friend's voice can sound almost as if it's next door? That's in part because telephone lines are designed to handle the narrow dynamic range of the human voice, not the wide dynamic range of music.

streamable. Compression in the context of audio optimization means turning down the loudest portions of the file, in effect narrowing the dynamic range. And you set the parameters. Compression lessens the chance your audio may sound distorted at the loudest points. Compressed audio also just sounds better.

Open up your audio editing software and the audio file you captured in Chapter 2. Find the function called "Compression" or sometimes "Dynamics Compression." To apply it, you'll probably need to highlight all or portions of the waveform (the squiggly line giving a visual representation of the audio). Most editing software packages offer compression presets, so you don't have to spend a lot of time figuring out the right settings. If you want to play with these settings (recommended!), try these:

- Threshold: −10db
- Ratio: 4:1
- Attack and Release: 100ms
- Input level: 3db of compression
- Output level: 0db of compression

As always, use your ears to judge the results. If you don't like them, change the settings, or go with a preset. Always remember to listen to your results in headphones that block outside noise. At least listen to the results in high-quality speakers. Most music engineers carry personal speakers with them to each studio. They give them the cool name of "monitors."

Normalization

Streaming audio files sound best when they are loudest without distortion, sometimes called "clipping." "Normalizing" your audio file turns up the volume

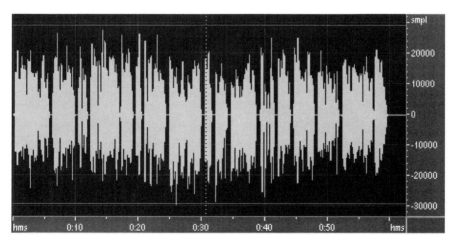

Figure 3.4 An example of dynamic range as seen in editing software (CoolEdit).

on the entire file to a point just before distortion occurs. Check your audio editing software for a Normalize function and normalize the file to about 95 percent, or −0.5dB. Keeping normalization just under 100 percent or 0dB gives the editing and encoding software a bit of wiggle room.

DC Offset

Inaudible noise is sometimes introduced into audio when the recording equipment isn't grounded properly. Your editing software's DC Offset function can remove this problem. Some software packages can remove this problem as you capture audio. Check your manual.

Noise Reduction

Many people have heard of noise reduction. Dolby Laboratories seems to have cornered the noise reduction market; there's even a Dolby button on some cheapo car stereos. In simplest terms, noise reduction (Dolby's and everyone else's) identifies unwanted audio frequencies and through complex calculations attenuates them without affecting the rest of the audio. In order to apply noise reduction to your audio file, pick a portion with just the unwanted sound, highlight it, analyze it, and create a profile. Then apply the profile to the entire file. Check your editing software manual for the specifics.

Use noise reduction carefully. It requires some advanced understanding of acoustics to get good results. If you're unsure, use equalization only.

Optimize Your Video

Video capturing is an inexact science, and you may find unwanted artifacts or other problems with the video image once you have it on your hard drive. At the very least, the video probably doesn't start or end exactly where you want. You may see black bars along the edges. Or the video seems too dark or too bright. Now is the time to optimize the video. (Note that the audio optimizations above apply to audio tracks in video as well.)

Unfortunately, video files are not as plastic as audio files. This is why correct capturing technique is so important. Video has fewer "fixes" available to it than audio. But there are a few things you can do.

First, let's quickly review some good video capture settings from Chapter 2:

- Frame size: 320 × 240
- Frame rate: 30 fps (frames per second)
- Compression ratio: Lowest available

Once you get some experience, you might play with these settings a bit. You might try capturing at a larger frame size, say 640 × 480. (Remember to use a 4:3 ratio!) This is useful if you plan to stream at very high bit rates. But the bigger frame doubles your file size more or less. And you should attempt to capture uncompressed video. This means you'll have all the video information you could possibly need. But the file size will be enormous, and you will quickly eat up disk storage space. Furthermore, capturing at a large frame size requires a more powerful computer, or else you could lose video frames. Try it, but if you drop more than a few frames, go back to the smaller frame size.

As with audio, we recommend following a certain order in your video optimizations to get the most out of them. The order isn't hard and fast, though.

✓ Editing
✓ Cropping
✓ Video processing
✓ Filtering
✓ Resizing
✓ Rendering

Editing

Editing moving images is an art form. It's not as simple as removing an "ahh" or an "umm." When you take out an "aah," the two pieces of audio on either side simply come together and the listener is none the wiser. But when you cut out a piece from a moving image, you wind up with something called a "jump cut." The eye will notice that something is missing, even if the change is slight. The worst of these edits will break up the rhythm of the video, causing viewers to say unconsciously to themselves, "What was that?" Now you've lost the viewer's full attention.

A simple solution to the jump cut problem is a "cutaway." When you're shooting your video, spend a few minutes recording some of the visual information around you. These could include shots of the audience, other participants

Figure 3.5   Using a covering shot to mask a jump cut.

in an event, or the general scene where the action takes place. These are called "covering shots." At your workstation, capture some of this video, using the same settings as your main video. When you come across a jump cut, take a piece of a covering shot, and "cover" the jump cut with the visual image, while maintaining the original audio. This takes some practice, but the transition will be much smoother and less likely to confuse the audience.

TV News and Covering Shots

Television news editors use covering shots constantly. Next time you watch the evening news, look for a story about a speech or a press conference. You might see video of the speaker delivering an announcement or answering a question. Suddenly, the shot changes to one of all the cameras and their operators recording the event. Then the shot changes to the speaker again. Chances are the editor used a covering shot of the cameras to mask a jump cut. He or she may also have used the shot to give the scene a bit of variety in case the particular image or content was dull.

Use the video editing process to add simple effects. For example, it's a good idea to fade up from black at the beginning of a video and fade down to black at the end. This transition signals visually the beginning and end of a video. You can also add simple titles, called "slides," at the beginning and credits at the end. (Don't forget to give yourself credit!) However, you should avoid the temptation to add a lot of effects that introduce too much information to the video file, such as wipes, whip pans, fast dissolves, etc. These generally don't translate well to streaming media, especially at low bit rates. To add visual effects, check your editing software manual for the exact procedures.

Cropping

If you have done any kind of photography beyond snapshots, you've probably cropped an image or two. Perhaps you needed to remove Aunt Argyle from the edge of a family portrait, because she's cut you out of her will. You probably used your photo manipulation software's cropping tool to symbolically, uh, punish her. (Sounds like you need therapy, my friend.)

Streaming media producers use the cropping functions of video editing software to solve two less emotional problems, overscan and letterboxing.

Overscan

When you capture a video image, you may notice black bars around the edges of the image. These bars are normally covered by the plastic casing around a television's picture tube. Obviously, you don't need these bars, which are called "overscan."

To solve this problem, use your editing software's cropping function. In many editing tools, video cropping works very much like the cropping tool in photograph manipulation software. Simply draw a rectangle inside the video image that leaves out the overscan area.

WARNING! Did we say "simply"? Well, it ain't so simple. You need to make sure the pixel dimensions of the new rectangle sans overscan match the 4:3 ratio of the original video dimensions. This means for every 4 pixels you shave off the width, you need to take 3 pixels off the height. Otherwise, your video could suffer distortion later in the process.

Letterboxing

Movies shot in a wide-screen format such as Cinemascope are sometimes shown on TV in their original aspect ratio. This means black bars appear on the top and bottom of the image. This is called "letterboxing."

In terms of streaming, these bars are just extra information you don't need to transmit over the Internet. Your viewers are better off without them. Use your video cropping tool to draw a square inside the actual image and lop off the unneeded bits. As with overscan, be sure your cropped image dimensions have a 4:3 ratio, or your image could become distorted later in the optimization process.

Video Processing

Television screens and computer screens use very different technologies to display images. Video looks generally darker on a computer screen than on a TV screen, and the colors and contrast usually look different as well.

Figure 3.6 Overscan and letterboxing. Overscan is the black area around the gray rectangles.

You'll remember our suggestion to buy a processing amplifier ("proc amp") in Chapter 2. These devices allow you to manipulate an incoming video signal. If you don't have a hardware proc amp, there's a good chance you can do similar manipulations using your video editing software. While hardware proc amps don't offer fine-grained control, software processing lets you change individual shots, even frames. The trick is to limit your urge to fix to the amount that gets the job done without introducing more problems.

The most likely change you'll make is brightness. As you play with it, you may notice your blacks moving closer to gray. You'll just have to fiddle with the settings until you like what you see. Check your editing software manual for specifics.

Filtering

Most editing software packages and later versions of some encoders contain filters that take out certain artifacts introduced by the capturing process. The filters we'll talk about are deinterlacing, inverse telecine, and noise reduction.

Deinterlacing

As mentioned above, TV monitors display visual data differently than computer monitors. Video equipment records data in a way meant for display on televisions. When the data is displayed on a computer screen, artifacts are introduced under certain circumstances. One artifact occurs when a portion of video data overlaps or interlaces with another, especially when images sizes are larger than 320 × 240 and there's a lot of movement in the frame. Use your editing software's deinterlacing filter to remove these artifacts.

Inverse Telecine

Motion picture film is usually shot at 24 fps. Video is shot at 30 fps. (Actually, it's 29.97 fps, but we won't be picky.) When film is transferred to video, the process introduces duplicate frames to make up the extra 6 frames per second. This is redundant information you don't need for streaming. Use your editing software package's inverse telecine filter to remove these extra frames. Then render the video as "non-progressive." This removes the problem from the final video file. (You'll need to review your editing software's instruction for specific steps related to rendering.)

Noise Reduction

Remember we recommended in Chapter 2 that you use the highest quality cameras and recording equipment you can. One reason is to reduce the chance for grainy pictures or general low quality. This "noise" can also appear as lines, snow, or any other unwanted electronic glitches. However, if you're trapped into using a cheap consumer video camera, you may be able to clean the image up a bit with your editing software's noise reduction. Be careful. Noise reduction may blur the image, introducing even more problems in an already problematic video image.

Rendering

The final step in the video optimization process is saving all the edits and optimizations into a file that will become your encoded streaming media. This is called "rendering." The most important rendering decision you'll make is image size. This should be the final size you want for the streamed image. You may decide to render two or more files, if you want one size for high-bandwidth users and a smaller size for low-bandwidth users. A large image is closer to the TV experience most users expect. A smaller image size might mean a sharper image. The type of content you have, e.g., talking heads or fast action, may also influence your decision. As we discussed in the section on cropping, make sure your image dimensions are in a ratio of 4:3. Here are some standard streaming video image sizes:

- 640 × 480 (recommended only for very high-bandwidth streaming)
- 320 × 240
- 240 × 180
- 176 × 132 (FYI: This is the current standard size for streaming over mobile networks.)

Now that you've optimized your video and chosen your image size, render your video. Depending on the length of the video and the power of your workstation, rendering could take 30 minutes or more. So take a break and get ready for encoding.

Testing Image Sizes

If you're unsure how the video will look at different image sizes, take a small portion of your video and create a new file. Then render and encode the sample. That will save time and energy.

Choosing the Right Codec

One of the first questions we get from people who've learned a little bit about streaming media is, "What codec should I use?" They often ask this question without thinking very much about the entire process, and not really understanding the place of codecs in the production stream. Codecs are also rather mysterious and slightly scary. Some people say it means enCOde/DECode. Others say it means COmpress/DECompress. Even the word "codec" has a certain Klingon-dialect feel to it.

These perceptions are probably the fault of the vendors, who compete strenuously on the quality of these critical components of their streaming systems. They spend large amounts of money researching or buying the rights to use these algorithms, which become massively hyped points of differentiation. In other words, the competition sometimes boils down to "Our codec is better than his codec." Codecs are also a way of tying a customer to a particular system. Once a producer settles on a vendor's proprietary codecs, it's hard to move to another vendor. The switching costs are just too big.

It's important to keep codecs in perspective. You're correct if you understand the central importance of codec choice. We'll discuss how to make that choice in this section. But, hopefully, you've gathered from the rest of this book up to this point that codecs are only one piece of a bigger puzzle. Don't get hung up on them.

What We Perceive and What Codecs Do

Streaming media is just one of many ways producers can deliver sound and light to an audience. Professionals in every medium, from music to painting to film-making to codec engineering, start with research into the way humans perceive sound and light. Without this knowledge, codec design would be impossible.

Sound

Humans hear sound in the range of 20 Hz (low) to 20,000 Hz (high). Information on either side of this range is inaudible. Musical tones can take up a large portion of the audible spectrum. The range of a human voice is far narrower, from about 500 Hz to 2,000 Hz. Vowels tend to take up most of the low range. Consonants take up the higher frequencies.

You'll see audio codecs roughly divided into music and voice, because of the different characteristics. Codecs work by removing information irrelevant to the perceptual experience of sound. These codecs are referred to as "lossy," because information is "lost" in the encoding process. (Codecs that don't lose information are called "lossless.") Lossy audio codecs first remove information below 20 Hz and above 20,000 Hz. Music codecs take out more information, but not as much as voice-only codecs. The latter can throw away large amounts of information, because of the narrow range of human speech. Voice codecs were among the first truly successful codecs, because you could transmit very high-quality speech sounds over dialup Internet connections.

Light and Motion

Light and color are central to the human experience. Our eyes are especially tuned to motion, which is one reason why action movies can be so riveting. The amount of data the millions of rods and cones in our retinas gather and send to the brain is almost beyond comprehension. In fact, the brain can't handle it all, and we've evolved internal filters to help us decide which data to pay attention to and which to ignore.

Lossy video codecs attempt to do something similar. Because the Internet cannot handle the sheer number of bits in an uncompressed video file, codecs look for information that's redundant and gets rid of it. In conventional film or video, the information in each frame replaces the information in the previous frame. But much of this information is the same, frame to frame. Maybe it's the color of the sky or the lamp in the background. Instead of replacing all the information frame to frame, codecs replace only the parts that change. Every few seconds, a codec inserts a "key frame," which becomes a reference point until another key frame appears. (The other frames are called "difference frames," because they only contain information different from the key frames.)

Video codecs can be roughly divided into two kinds, low action and high action. Low-action codecs are designed for video with little movement in the frame, such as a speech or a "talking heads" program. They have fewer key frames and large amounts of repeated information, such as a background blue screen. Low-action codecs can work well at dialup speeds. High-action codecs, on the other hand, have more key frames and less repeated information frame to frame. These codecs are designed for music videos or movie trailers. They work best on high bit rate connections, at least cable/DSL.

What We Mean by "Codec"

In Chapter 2, we discussed a number of different source file types, such as WAV for audio and AVI (or MOV) for video. These files are also created by codecs, but not streaming media codecs. In this book, we use the term "codec" to refer to mathematical formulas that transform source files to streamable files.

Proprietary and "Standards-Based" Codecs

Codecs can also be divided into proprietary and "standards-based." As we discussed above, streaming media vendors compete to offer the best

Continued

audio and video codecs. They guard the codec designs jealously, because these formulas are built as competitive advantages. They also tie ("ensnare" is perhaps a better word) a customer to the vendor's products.

Standards-based codecs, sometimes called open codecs, are based on publicly agreed-on technical principles, which a company or individual may or may not own. Streams encoded with these codecs can play, theoretically, across multiple platforms. The best known of these standards in the context of streaming is MPEG-4. Of course, vendors have to decide to support open standards, which could mean loss of a competitive advantage. We'll hear more about MPEG-4 and open standards in Chapter 5.

Making the Choice

Which codec do you use? You should first analyze your content. What types of information does it contain? Audio content is relatively easy to analyze. When you deconstruct video content, you'll analyze a video track and an audio track, and you'll apply the results of your audience analysis conducted in the first part of this chapter. The answers to the questions below should help you make a final choice.

- Is the audio primarily voice, music, or a mixture of voice and music? If it's a mixture, is the music just for variety or is it critical to the message?
- Is the video primarily one or two people speaking, such as a lecture or panel discussion, with only a few scene changes?
- Does the video contain numerous scene changes or lots of movement in the frame, such as music video or an action thriller movie?
- What streaming platform and Internet connection speed do you expect for your target audience?

Your choice of a streaming platform may limit your codec choices by default. The RealNetworks RealPlayer Helix platform is the most flexible; the latest versions can stream and play almost all known forms of audio and visual media. If you choose Windows Media, your codecs are limited to those supported by Microsoft. Same with Apple QuickTime and Macromedia Flash MX.

If you have the resources, we suggest you encode in at least two of the four major formats, especially if you can't be sure which media players the audience will use. Chances are, a home user or small-business person can play streams of at least one of the two platforms you choose.

OK, you say, you've laid out how to make a decision. Now tell me the decision to make. Sorry, we can't do that. It's almost impossible to cover all the possible combinations of circumstances that might lead you to select one codec or another. There are dozens of codecs to choose from, all with unique characteristics. Fortunately, today's encoding tools make codec selection relatively easy. They'll help with automatic selections for certain circumstances, and you should always experiment in unfamiliar situations. (We'll learn more encoding tools later in this chapter.)

The thing to remember is this: Codecs are just like wrenches in a toolbox. You have to apply brainpower to get any value out of them. Ultimately, you have to apply your own sense of what works and what doesn't work to the technology at hand. Always trust your own judgment, and fearlessly wield the tools to implement your vision.

Media Player Behavior and Multiple Bit Rate Encoding

We have to cover one more set of principles before we get to the actual encoding. Most media players behave in similar ways that every streaming media user experiences. Some of these behaviors can be very frustrating. Fortunately, you can mitigate some of the frustration with good encoding practices. This section explains some of the behaviors and a suggested solution.

Pre-Roll

When your end-user at home or in the next cubicle clicks a link to a streaming media file, the media player attempts to contact the streaming media server to get the stream. The player shows this by displaying a "Connecting . . ." or similar message. A logo may spin or flash as well. When the connection occurs, the player may then say "Buffering . . ." or "Loading . . .." This could go on for several seconds or longer, depending on the connection speed, the network conditions, and player settings.

Here's what's happening. The player is filling a reservoir of random access memory (RAM) with data from the stream. When the reservoir is filled, the audio or video starts to play. In the meantime, the player continues to receive

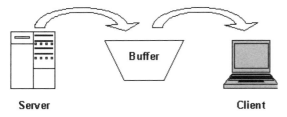

Server   Client

Figure 3.7 A media player keeps a buffer of memory filled with streaming data to maintain a smooth user experience.

data from the streaming server. It tries to keep the reservoir, also called the "buffer," filled so that playback continues without interruption, creating a smooth user experience from the beginning of the clip to the end.

Rebuffering

The unpredictability of the Internet can sabotage a player's valiant attempt at smooth playback. One minute, network conditions may be perfect. The next minute, something in the great cloud goes haywire and the media player stops receiving data from the streaming server. The media buffer empties, and playback stops while the player asks the server for more data to refill the buffer. The player tells the user what's going on by redisplaying a "Buffering . . ." or "Loading . . ." message. As with pre-roll, rebuffering can seem to take forever.

You can't control net weather, at least for users outside your own network. However, you can mitigate the problem with "multiple bit rate" encoding. This means combining several bit rates into a single encoded file. For example, if you combine encoding settings for a 56 kbps dialup connection with settings for a 256 kbps cable/DSL connection, the player will ask the server for the version that fits the current network conditions. The player will shift up or down depending on its needs. Note that a downshift could cause a loss in quality because 56 kbps streams carry much less data than a higher bit rate stream.

Another caveat: For this scenario to work, the player has to know via its own settings that it's on a cable/DSL connection so that it can shift up or down as needed. If it's set to receive streams for a dialup connection only, it will never ask for the 256 kbps stream.

Encoding

Now we come to the part you've all been waiting for: encoding. All your preparation of the audio or video file will now pay off with a high-quality encoded file that will reflect the high quality of your original work. We'll take you step-by-step through the encoding process for each of the four major vendors: RealNetworks, Microsoft, Apple, and Macromedia.

If you haven't done so already, download and install the free RealNetworks RealProducer Basic and the Microsoft Windows Media Encoder. You will need to purchase an Apple QuickTime Pro license to encode with the QuickTime Player. You can encode for Macromedia Flash MX with the evaluation version of Flash MX. You might want to review the basic encoding procedures in Chapter 1 as well. We'll assume you have a `.wav` file and/or an `.avi` file as your source file.

> ## Tell the User about Title, Author, and Copyright
>
> All of the major encoders let you add title, author, copyright, and description information to the encoded file. This is an obvious feature, but often overlooked. The title, author, and copyright information usually appears in the media player as it's playing, giving users crucial information. Keyword and description data may also help you identify and index files later, especially if you encode large amounts of material.

Encode Your Audio

RealNetworks RealProducer Basic Step-by-Step:

1. Open RealProducer Basic.
2. Make sure the Input File radio button is selected.
3. Click the Browse button.
4. Highlight the file you wish to encode and click Open.
5. Click the Audiences button.
6. In the dialog box, select the Audio Mode appropriate for your content from the drop-down menu.
7. Select No Video from the Video Mode drop-down menu.

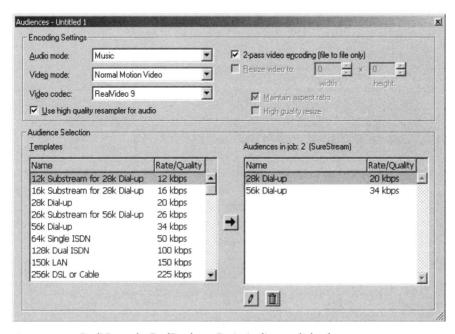

Figure 3.8 RealNetworks RealProducer Basic Audiences dialog box.

8. In the Audiences in Job box, note the audiences already listed. These are the different bandwidths targeted by you.
    a. If you want to remove any audiences from the list, highlight the item with your mouse, and click the Trash icon below the box.
    b. If you want to add any audiences, highlight one of the items in the Templates box and click the arrow. This will add the audience to the audiences list.
9. Close the Audiences dialog box by clicking the "X" in the upper right corner.
10. Click the Clip Information button and fill in Title, Author, Copyright, Keyword, and Description information. Also, choose a rating for your encoded file from the drop-down menu.
11. Close the Clip Information dialog box by click the "X" in the upper right corner.
12. Note the file name in the Destinations box. This will be the name of your file once it's encoded. It will be placed in the same directory as your source file.
13. To change the name of the encoded file and its destination, click the Pencil icon or right-click the default file name and select Edit Destination.
14. If you are satisfied with your settings, click the Encode button.
15. When encoding is complete, click the RealOne logo under the Destination box to play the file. Or open the file in your RealPlayer. The file will begin playing.

Advanced Settings in RealProducer

To see further options for each audience in RealProducer, highlight one of your audience selections, and click the Pencil icon next to the Trash icon. The paid version of RealProducer allows you to modify audio and video codecs and other parameters for these audience settings. You can also create custom templates. These features and others are not available in the free RealProducer.

Windows Media Encoder Step-by-Step:

To understand more about the details of Windows Media, we'll create a custom session, rather than using a wizard, as we did in Chapter 1.

1. Open Windows Media Encoder by clicking Start->Programs->Windows Media->Windows Media Encoder.
2. In the wizards dialog box, select Custom Session. Click OK.

3. In the Session Properties window, click the File radio button.
4. Click the Browse button and select the audio file you wish to encode.
5. Click the Output tab.
6. Check the Archive to File checkbox.
7. Enter a file name for your encoded file.
8. Click the Compression tab.
9. Select "Windows Media Server (streaming)" from the Destination drop-down menu.
10. Select "Multiple bit rates (audio)" from the Audio drop-down menu.

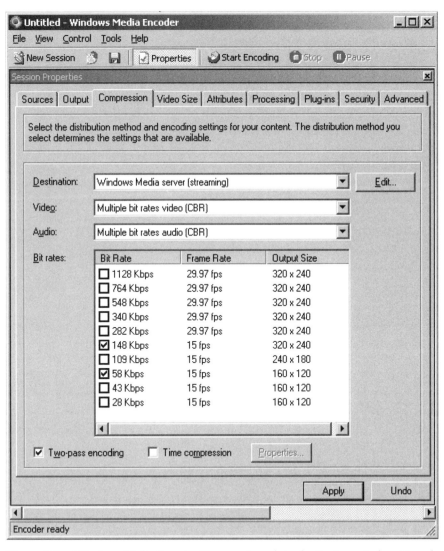

Figure 3.9 Windows Media Encoder Compression tab in the Sessions window. Note the bit rate selections for a multiple bit rate encoding.

11. Choose the bit rates of your target audience from the "Bit rates" box.
12. Click the Attributes tab.
13. Select the Title, Author, Copyright, Rating, and Description fields and click Edit to add the appropriate information.
14. If you are satisfied with your settings, click the Apply button.
15. Click the Start Encoding button to start the encoding.
16. When the Encoding Results dialog box appears, click the Play Output File button to review the encoded file.
17. Click the Close button to end the encoding session.

Custom Compression Profiles

Windows Media Encoder allows you to create custom audio compression profiles for later re-use. To create a profile, click the Edit button next to the Destination drop-down menu under the Compression tab in the Session window. Change the parameters as needed, and give the profile a descriptive name to help you identify it later. Click Export and give the new profile a file name.

Windows Media Encoder also has a number of ready-to-go profiles. To use one of these, click Import and select one of the profiles. You'll also use the Import function to retrieve your own custom profiles.

Apple Computer QuickTime Pro Encoding Step-by-Step

1. Open QuickTime Player.
2. Select File->Open Movie in New Player.
3. Find the directory where your audio file is located.
4. If it is not displayed in the directory, select "Audio files" from the Files of Type drop-down menu.
5. Select your audio file and click Convert.
6. Select File->Export. (If you do not see the Export menu item, you will need to purchase a QuickTime Pro license and install it to encode with QuickTime Player.)
7. Choose "Export to QuickTime Movie" from the Export drop-down menu. (Even though your file is audio only, it is referred to as a "movie" by QuickTime.)
8. In the Use drop-down menu, select your target audience.
9. Click the Options button to open the Movie Settings dialog box.
10. Click the Settings button under the Sound checkbox.

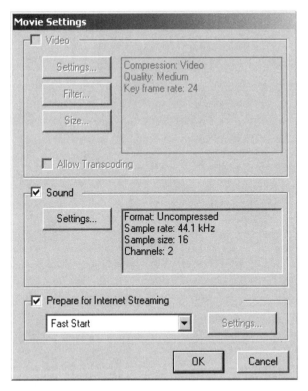

Figure 3.10 QuickTime Pro Movie Settings dialog box. Since the file is audio only, the video section is grayed out.

11. In the Sound Settings window, select a codec in the Compressor drop-down menu. Your options may change depending on the codec you choose.
12. Click OK.
13. Check the Prepare for Internet Streaming check box.
14. Select Hinted Streaming from the drop-down menu.
15. Click Settings.
16. Check the Make Movie Self-Contained checkbox and click OK.
17. Click OK in the Movie Settings dialog box.
18. Click Save in the Save Exported File As dialog box and encoding will begin.
19. In the QuickTime Player, select File -> Open Movie in New Player.
20. Select the new audio `.mov` file, and click the Play button. The newly encoded file should start playing.

Macromedia Flash MX Encoding Step-by-Step
1. Start Macromedia Flash MX.
2. Create a new animation project.

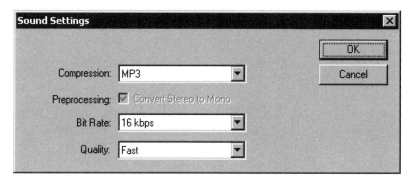

Figure 3.11 Macromedia Flash MX Sound Settings dialog box.

3. Create an audio layer.
4. Select File->Import to Library and find your audio file in your working directory. Click Open. Your audio file is added to your Library.
5. Select a Key Frame for the audio.
6. In the Properties panel, click the Sound drop-down menu and select your audio file.
7. In the Properties panel, click the Sync drop-down menu and select Stream.
8. Click File->Publish Settings and select the Flash (`.swf`) Type.
9. Uncheck the Use Default Names checkbox and give the file a name.
10. Click on the Flash Tab. Make sure Compress Movie is checked.
11. Select the Flash Version you wish to target from the drop-down menu.
12. Click the Set button next to the Audio Stream listing.
13. Select the Compression Type from the drop-down menu.
14. Select the Bit Rate from the drop-down menu according to the bandwidth of your target audience.
15. Click OK.
16. Click Publish. A file with the `.swf` extension will be created in the directory where you normally publish (save) your `.swf` files. To play the file, open it with your Web browser. Remember, Flash is played via a plug-in in your browser.

A Bit More About Encoder Features

The streaming media encoders discussed in this chapter have many more features than can be explained in a book geared toward beginning and intermediate streaming producers. The number and type of features vary from encoder to encoder, but they fall into a number of categories.

Here are a few of those categories. We urge you to explore them as your skill and knowledge improves.

Live streaming: RealNetworks RealProducer and Microsoft Windows Media Encoder allow you to capture a live audio or video signal and encode it as a live stream. (Apple also has a live streaming encoder, but it's not part of QuickTime Player or QuickTime Pro. The Macromedia Flash MX creation tool does not contain a live streaming feature.) Sometimes called "webcasting," live streaming has its own unique demands. But it's one of the fastest growing aspects of the streaming media business.

Variable Bit Rates: Most of the encoding discussed in this book follows the "constant bit rate" model. That is, when a bit rate is negotiated by the media player and the server, the rate generally remains constant. In the case of "multiple bit rate" encoding, the media player and server shift among two or more constant bit rates embedded in the streaming file. In "variable bit rate" encoding, the bit rate is more fluid, especially when the content changes in quality, such as low-motion to high-motion. Variable bit rate is used most often in non-streaming scenarios, such as playing movies off a CD-ROM or DVD. Encoders include it because some producers use encoding tools for more than just Internet streaming.

Digital Rights Management (DRM): Streaming media vendors have developed encryption systems to protect the intellectual property of copyright owners. DRM tools embed protections, sometimes called watermarks, that prevent unauthorized copying or other access to streaming media files.

If you'd like to learn more about these features, visit the vendors' websites or check the encoders' online help files.

Table 3.3. Common file extensions for streaming media files. Use these extensions to recognize the systems used to encode a file

Vendor	File Extension
RealNetworks	`.ra, .rm`
Microsoft	`.asf, .wma, .wmv`
Apple Computer	`.mov`
Macromedia	`.swf`

Encode Your Video

Most of the steps for video encoding are the same as audio encoding above. Remember, streaming video is actually two streams, audio and video, that run synchronously. In video encoding, you make choices for your video stream as well as your audio stream.

RealNetworks RealProducer Basic Encoding Step-by-Step

1. Open RealProducer Basic.
2. Make sure the Input File radio button is selected.
3. Click the Browse button.
4. Highlight the file you wish to encode and click Open.
5. Click the Audiences button.
6. In the dialog box, select the Audio Mode appropriate for your content from the drop-down menu.
7. Select the Video Mode appropriate for your content from the drop-down menu.

RealProducer's Video Mode Choices

The RealNetworks RealProducer Basic offers the streaming media producer four Video Mode choices: Normal Motion Video, Sharpest Image, Smoothest Motion, Slide Show, and No Video. These affect the quality of the image, no matter the video codec.

- *Normal Motion Video* is for clips with the widest range of motion.
- *Sharpest Image* keeps the image sharper, but at a lower frame rate.
- *Smoothest Motion* keeps the motion smoother, but at the cost of image clarity.
- *Slide Show* creates the illusion of numerous still photos.
- *No Video* is for stripping the audio track off a video file.

---

8. Note that the Video Codec drop-down menu is defaulted to RealVideo 9. If you want more choices, you will need to buy the full version of RealProducer. *Warning*: Using RealVideo 9 means RealPlayer users with older RealPlayers may not be able to play your video. If they try to play video encoded with RealVideo 9 codecs, the media player may ask them to upgrade. Consult your audience analysis for guidance on whether your audience is tolerant of the "hassle factor."
9. Check the 2-Pass Video Encoding checkbox. "2-pass encoding" means the encoder will analyze the file once for the optimal application of the codec. Then the encoder applies the codec on the second pass.

10. In the Audiences in Job box, note the audiences already listed. These are the different bandwidths targeted by you.
    a. If you want to remove any audiences from the list, highlight the item with your mouse, and click the Trash icon below the box.
    b. If you want to add any audiences, highlight one of the items in the Templates box and click the arrow. This will add the audience to the audiences list.
11. Close the Audiences dialog box by clicking the "X" in the upper right corner.

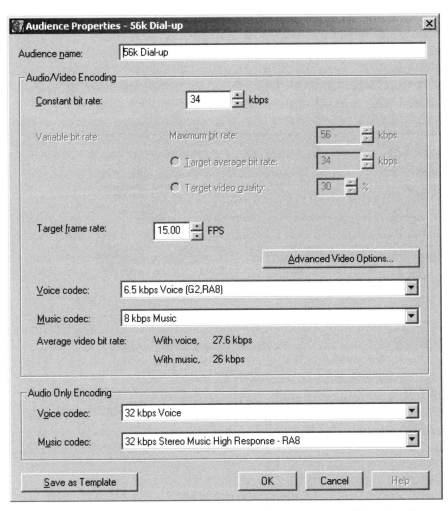

Figure 3.12 RealNetworks RealProducer Basic Audiences Properties dialog box. You can display the audience properties by highlighting one of your target audiences in the Audiences in Job box, such as "56K dialup." However, RealProducer Basic users will not be able to modify the settings.

12.   Click the Clip Information button and fill in Title, Author, Copyright, Keyword, and Description information. Also, choose a rating for your encoded file from the drop-down menu.

13.   Close the Clip Information dialog box by clicking the "X" in the upper right corner.

14.   Note the file name in the Destinations box. This will be the name of your file once it's encoded. It will be placed in the same directory as your source file.

15.   To change the name of the encoded file and its destination, click the Pencil icon or right-click the default file name and select Edit Destination.

16.   If you are satisfied with your settings, click the Encode button.

17.   When encoding is complete, click the RealOne logo under the Destination box to play the file. Or open the file in your RealPlayer. The file will begin playing.

Should You Use Image Manipulation Features in the Encoders?

The encoders from the three leading streaming media vendors, RealNetworks, Microsoft, and Apple Computer, offer options such as image resizing, cropping, de-interlacing, and inverse telecine. Ideally, you should take care of all these items in the source file *before* you encode. That gives you maximum control over the final output, and it limits the encoder to its true job: encoding files for streaming. But you may find these options useful if you have no time to fix the issues in the source file. You can also experiment, and see if you get better results by resizing, for example, in your encoder rather than your video editing application.

Windows Media Encoder Step-by-Step

We'll create a custom video encoding session, rather than using a wizard, just as we did in the audio encoding session above.

1.   Open Windows Media Encoder by clicking Start->Programs-> Windows Media->Windows Media Encoder.

2.   In the wizards dialog box, select Custom Session. Click OK.

3.   In the Session Properties window, click the File radio button.

4.   Click the Browse button and select the video file you wish to encode.

5.   Click the Output tab.

6.   Check the Archive to File checkbox.

7. Uncheck all other options.
8. Enter a file name for your encoded file.
9. Click the Compression tab.
10. Select "Windows Media Server (streaming)" from the Destination drop-down menu.
11. Select "Multiple bit rates (video)" from the Video drop-down menu.
12. Select "Multiple bit rates (audio)" from the Audio drop-down menu.
13. Choose the bit rates of your target audience from the "Bit rates" box.

Customizing Windows Media Encoder Settings

Windows Media Encoder allows you to customize numerous encoding settings. Here's how to do this:

1. In the Compression tab, check the bit rate selections appropriate to your target audience.
2. Click the Edit button next to the Destination drop-down menu.
3. In the Custom Encoding Settings window (see Figure 3.13), you'll see a General tab and at least one other tab corresponding to your bit rate selection(s).
4. Click a bit rate selection tab. You'll find a number of options. The most important ones are the following:

- *Audio Format:* You can adjust the amount of bandwidth used by the audio track in your video. If you select a lower audio bit rate, you can assign more bits to the video track.
- *Frame Rate:* You'll sometimes see "29.97" as the frame rate. This is commonly referred to as "30 frames per second." ("29.97" is the rate specified by a television engineering group for analog video transmission.) You can often change this to 15 frames per second without losing too much image quality.
- *Video Bit Rate:* You can adjust the amount of bits used to transmit video data up or down, depending on your target. Make only small adjustments here. If large adjustments are called for, Cancel the dialog. Then go back to the Compression tab and select another bit rate.
- *Video Smoothness:* Adjust this number up or down to regulate the sharpness of the image. However, sharper images may mean jerky motion.
- *Key Frame Interval:* Modifying this number changes the number of seconds between each key frame. If you have a lot of motion, a lower number may be called for. But that will result

Continued

in a larger encoded file. However, don't wander too much from the defaults. You could cause more problems than you solve.

- *Total Bit Rate:* As you adjust the bit rate allocations, pay attention to the totals in the lower part of the window. This will help you track whether your final file will match the bandwidths of your target audience. Note also the Overhead total. This tells you that a portion of bandwidth is allocated to special kinds of data needed by the streaming server and media player to communicate efficiently and deliver the content reliably.

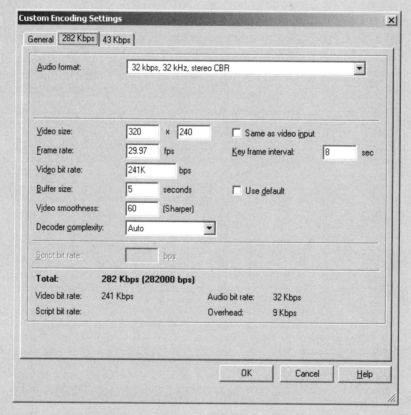

Figure 3.13 Windows Media Encoder Custom Encoding Settings window. In this example, you have three tabs: General, 282 Kbps (shown), and 43 Kbps. These bit rates could be selected for a user with a cable/DSL Internet connection or a dialup connection.

14. Check the "Two-Pass Encoding" check box. The encoder will look at the video twice: once to analyze it for optimal encoding, and a second time to apply the codec.
15. Click the Attributes tab.
16. Select the Title, Author, Copyright, Rating, and Description fields and click Edit to add the appropriate information.
17. If you are satisfied with your settings, click the Apply button.
18. Click the Start Encoding button to start the encoding.
19. When the Encoding Results dialog box appears, click the Play Output File button to review the encoded file.
20. Click the Close button to end the encoding session.

Apple Computer QuickTime Pro Encoding Step-by-Step

1. Open QuickTime Player.
2. Select File->Open Movie in New Player.
3. Find the directory where your video file is located.
4. Select your video file and click Convert.
5. If you have more than one QuickTime Player window open, you may want to close the others to avoid confusion.
6. Select File->Export. (If you do not see the Export menu item, you will need to purchase a QuickTime Pro license and install it to encode with QuickTime Player.)
7. Choose "Export Movie to QuickTime Movie" from the Export drop-down menu.
8. In the Use drop-down menu, select your target audience.
9. Click the Options button to open the Movie Settings dialog box.
10. Click the Settings button under the Video checkbox.
11. In the Compression Settings window, select a codec from the drop-down menu. Your other options in this window may change depending on the selected codec.
12. Select a video quality by moving the slider.
13. Choose a frames-per-second value by clicking the arrow next to the Frames Per Second text box.
14. Modify the "Key frame every" text box as needed.
15. Click OK.
16. In the Movie Settings window, click the Filter button under the Video checkbox.
17. In the Choose Video Filter window, you'll note several options. Depending on the codec, you may be able to modify the sharpness of the video image. Look for this option, and change as needed. (For more information on sharpness vs. smoothness, see the RealNetworks RealProducer Basic and Windows Media Encoder procedures above.)
18. Click OK.

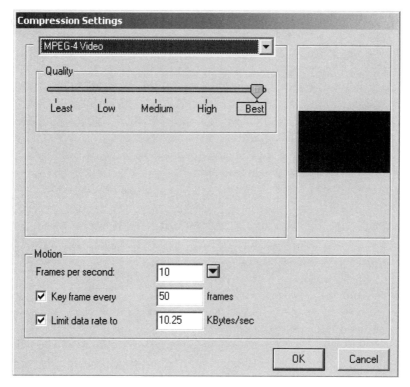

Figure 3.14   QuickTime Pro Compression Settings dialog box.

19. In the Movie Settings window, click the Settings button under the Sound checkbox.

20. In the Sound Settings window, select a codec in the Compressor drop-down menu. Your options may change depending on the codec you choose.

21. Click OK.

22. Check the Prepare for Internet Streaming check box.

23. Select Hinted Streaming from the drop-down menu.

24. Click Settings.

25. Check the Make Movie Self-Contained checkbox and click OK.

26. Click OK in the Movie Settings dialog box.

27. Click Save in the Save Exported File As dialog box and encoding will begin.

28. In the QuickTime Player, select File->Open Movie in New Player.

29. Select the new audio `.mov` file, and click the Play button. The newly encoded file should start playing.

Macromedia Flash MX Encoding Step-by-Step

1. Start Flash MX.

2. Open your animation project.

3. Select File->Import and find your video file in your working directory. Click Open.
4. In the Import Video window, select "Embed video in Macromedia Flash document." Click OK.
5. Use the Quality slider to adjust the sharpness or smoothness of the image. (For more information on sharpness vs. smoothness, see the procedures for RealNetworks RealProducer Basic and Windows Media Encoder procedures above.)
6. Use the Key Frame Interval slider to set the number of seconds between key frames. (See above procedures for more information on key frame intervals.)
7. Use the Scale slider to adjust the image size.
8. Check the Synchronize Video to Macromedia Flash Document Frame Rate checkbox
9. Check the Import Audio checkbox.
10. Click OK.

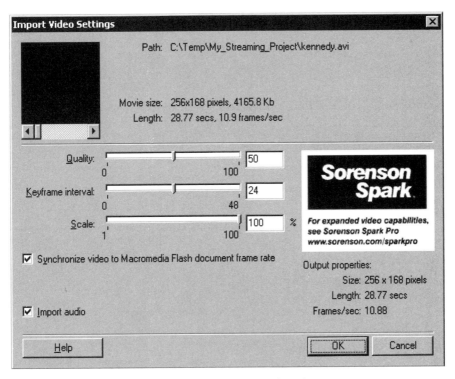

Figure 3.15 Macromedia Flash MX import settings for video.

Flash MX and Sorenson Codecs

Macromedia Flash MX uses only one codec, Sorenson Spark. If you'd like to try more Sorenson codecs, visit the Sorenson Media website at http://www.sorenson.com

11. You may be asked to let Flash MX increase the number of frames to the length required. Click OK.
12. Click File->Publish Settings and select the Flash (`.swf`) Type.
13. Uncheck the Use Default Names checkbox and give the file a name.
14. Click on the Flash tab. Make sure Compress Movie is checked.
15. Select the Flash Version you wish to target from the drop-down menu.
16. Click the Set button next to the Audio Stream listing.
17. Select the Compression Type from the drop-down menu.
18. Select the Bit Rate from the drop-down menu according to the bandwidth of your target audience.
19. Click OK.
20. Click Publish. A file with the `.swf` extension will be created in the directory where you normally publish (save) your `.swf` files. To play the file, open it with your Web browser. Remember, Flash is played via a plug-in in your browser.

Chapter Summary

We started this chapter by discussing important aspects of streaming media platforms and the place of these platforms in your decision making. We advised you to perform a careful analysis of your audience and suggested several aspects to examine. We talked about some methods for optimizing your audio and video source files in preparation for encoding. Finally, we spent time going over various encoding parameters and procedures for each of the major vendors.

The New World of Mobile Streaming Media

By John Shay
The world is witnessing the emergence of third-generation (3G) mobile networks capable of delivering vast quantities of data and multimedia

content to handheld consumer devices. Mobile networks are evolving from narrowband, circuit-switched networks, used primarily for voice and text, to broadband, packet-switched networks capable of delivering a broad range of Internet-like media services. Compared to today's 2G (voice plus text messaging) and 2.5G (voice plus text and picture messaging) networks, 3G mobile networks represent a profound leap in mobile communications.

A Paradigm Shift

Multimedia-capable mobile networks signal a paradigm shift within the telecommunications industry. The shift is most evident in the growing numbers of cell phones shipping with embedded cameras. Cameraphones designed for 2.5G networks enable consumers to send messages containing both pictures and text. Some observers predict cameraphones will outsell standard still cameras in 2004 (See graph).

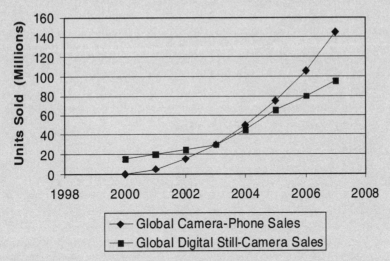

Source: Strategy Analytics, www.strategyanalytics.com

The ability to communicate in both words and pictures is a classic killer application.

3G Up and Running

Several 3G networks are running in Europe and Asia. The majority of 3G phones sold there come equipped with multiple cameras supporting

Continued

real-time, person-to-person video calling and video messaging. Video calling allows callers to see each other during the course of a call. Video messaging allows subscribers to record and share brief video clips.

State-of-the-art 3G cellular networks, principally owned by Hutchinson Whampoa Ltd. were recently launched in Europe, Hong Kong, and Australia that provide hints at the approaching paradigm shift. The service, called "3," markets itself as "The Mobile Video Company." Subscribers place international video calls, send video messages, and access popular video content including sport highlights, music videos, news and weather, and movie trailers. NTT DoCoMo in Japan offers a similar service. In the United States, 3G networks are being developed by AT&T and others. Some expect to begin 3G services by the fall of 2004.

Mobile Streaming's Unique Challenges

Although basic streaming concepts apply to mobile networks, the large and rapidly expanding variety of handsets coupled with the complex nature of mobile networks offer unique technological challenges.

Internet content providers generally assume that anyone browsing a streaming media website today has a Microsoft Windows-based PC or a Macintosh with a media player, a powerful processor, plenty of memory, and a color monitor. Nothing of the sort can be assumed about end-user devices on a mobile network. Mobile devices vary widely in terms of processor power, memory, operating system, protocol support, client software, screen size, and color depth. And the vast majority of mobile phones capable of playing streaming video do not support the leading proprietary Internet formats offered today by RealNetworks and Microsoft.

The only common video format supported by all 3G phones is MPEG4. Support for MPEG4 is mandated by the 3GPP, the leading industry standards body for 3G devices and networks. In addition to designating MPEG4 as the standard video format, the 3G industry has set media format standards regarding audio, graphics, and MIDI support. Standards have also been defined for both SMIL and XML layouts. To learn more about 3G standards, visit the 3GPP web site at www.3gpp.org. MPEG4 is discussed in detail in Chapter 5.

Hardware and Software Variables

The hardware and software variability between mobile devices also represents a significant challenge. Manufacturers introduce a new crop of mobile devices every few months, offering the latest in style and features. Although screen size and color display capabilities are the most obvious features subject to change, operating systems, processing power, memory, and media format support also play significant roles in regards to streaming media. Two companies, Vidiator Technology and Packet Video, have spent considerable resources on addressing device variability for mobile streaming media. Packet Video has focused on porting their software client to a wide selection of handsets and operating systems. Vidiator is working on enabling their server to *transcode* and *transform* streams to match the capabilities of the target device. Transcoding involves a format change, such as delivering a Windows Media video file as a 3GPP-compliant MPEG4 file. Transforming involves changing display characteristics of a file such as dimension, aspect ratio, pixel density, and color depth.

Another key difference between Internet and mobile streaming is that, by definition, devices on a mobile network enjoy freedom of movement. When a mobile device moves from one network cell to another, a complex handover procedure takes place that ensures that a continuous voice and data connections are maintained. The greatest challenge to streaming is not so much the handover itself, but the fact that bandwidth within a cell diminishes dramatically as one approaches the cell's edge. A subscriber's proximity to a cell tower can alter the data flow to a device and subsequently affect the quality of a streaming media experience. Two other factors affect bandwidth to a given device: 1) The number of devices operating simultaneously within a given cell and 2) the speed at which the device is traveling through the cell. Finally, high bandwidth coverage remains spotty within the streaming 3G networks, and seamless roaming between 3G networks will be problematic for the next year or two.

The telecommunications industry is on the cusp of a change comparable to the advent of streaming media in the mid-1990s. The change promises to be as interesting and exciting.

John Shay is a Director of International Business Development for Hutchison Whampoa Americas Ltd. Vidiator is a member of the Hutchison Whampoa Ltd. group of companies. John can be reached at johns@hwal.com.

4 Broadcast Your Audio and Video

Terms to Know

On-Demand: Most streaming media files are available "on-demand," meaning when the audience chooses to access them.

    Live: Streaming media produced at the same moment as the content is produced is usually called "live" streaming.

    Webcast: A live streaming media broadcast is sometimes called a "webcast," although the term is sometimes applied to on-demand streaming.

    Simultaneous streams: Streaming media producers often measure the popularity of a live stream by the number of simultaneous requests for the stream. One streaming software vendor also bases its streaming server license fees on the maximum number of simultaneous streams.

    Outsourcing: Many streaming producers prefer to hire out some or all of their streaming capacity to a streaming specialist. This is called "outsourcing."

Showing the World Your Work

Monday morning. Start of another work week. But instead of your usual depression, you're looking forward to the day. You've successfully encoded your source video file at your home workstation. The video image is sharp. The audio is clear. You understand your audience (attendees at the Las Vegas Hardware Hype and Vaporware Show) thoroughly. Now it's time to show them your work.

    In this chapter, we'll take you through the process of putting your streaming media before an audience. In some ways, this is the biggest challenge facing a streaming producer. You will have to work closely with the people who manage your organization's streaming server and network resources. Frankly, these professionals aren't always the most easygoing colleagues. Streaming media is a demanding technology, especially on bandwidth, which is the amount of data that can be transmitted over a network per second. Network and system administrators have to balance all the demands made on a network, and streaming can throw their systems out of kilter. Hopefully, you've explained your plans to your IT high priests from the beginning, so they can prepare for today, when you deliver your content. It's important to have them on your side throughout the process.

On the other hand, you may decide for a variety of reasons that your network can't handle your streaming needs. Maybe the network expertise you need isn't available in-house. Perhaps you don't have enough bandwidth for the traffic you expect. You have another option: outsourcing. Most independent web hosting companies have streaming servers you can "rent" for a monthly fee, just like website hosting. There are even a few companies that host streaming media exclusively. We'll discuss some criteria for choosing a streaming media hosting service at the end of the chapter.

Doing It Differently

This chapter is somewhat different than previous chapters. We won't show you how to install and configure a streaming server. Rather, we want to give you enough information to help you have intelligent conversations with network/system administrators. We want you to make good decisions about your infrastructure needs. Unless you're a server administrator/networking specialist, we think it's best for most streaming producers to leave the details of server and network configurations to the experts.

Home users and hobbyists: Frankly, unless you're a very serious hobbyist, you don't need to know a lot of the stuff in this chapter. You're better off checking with your Internet service provider about whether you have streaming media services as part of your account. If you do, then ask about how to set it up and use it. If you don't, you may have to think about switching providers if you really want to stream. (We hope so!) Then again, learning more behind-the-scenes stuff about Internet broadcasting might help you in the long run.

Live vs. On-Demand

Get Streaming: Quick Steps to Putting Your Audio and Video Online is designed with the intelligent beginner in mind. To keep things simple and straightforward, we decided to focus almost exclusively on the "on-demand" streaming option, that is, archiving streams for access whenever the audience chooses. That's why you've shot and encoded an on-demand file, the one that's in your hands right now.

But you may find yourself in the position of choosing whether to produce a live broadcast, as opposed to an on-demand broadcast. Or you may have to do both for the same content. Our advice: If you decide to produce live and you have little or no experience in producing live events, look seriously into outsourcing the project. Live events of all kinds, not just live streaming media broadcasts, have their own unique demands that go beyond the scope of this book and the abilities of most beginners, even smart ones. Nevertheless, we can help you decide whether your project is appropriate for a live broadcast or archiving for on-demand access.

When Should I Produce Live?

Live events are among the most exciting and compelling experiences we enjoy. It's fun to watch actors on a stage, because the action unfolds before your eyes. You know anything can happen, including the unexpected. Live broadcasting is similar. Ever wondered why television news departments go "live to the scene" whenever possible? Because a "live" storyteller (the reporter) adds an extra emotional edge, even drama, to a story when he or she tells it as it happens. That feeling is very hard to capture in a recording.

You should consider producing a live broadcast when you can capture and deliver action as it happens. You also need to judge whether the action, or the information delivered as part of the action, would have the most impact if delivered immediately, rather than at some later point. Here are some good candidates for a live streaming media broadcast:

- An annual address by a CEO or prominent political leader
- A new product rollout at an important industry conference
- An event where the outcome is uncertain, such as a game or debate

If you decide to produce an event live, you should probably double or triple your time and financial budgets, depending on the nature of the content. (A simple speech is easier to produce than a football game, for example.) Again, unless you have experience with live event or broadcast production, consider outsourcing part or all of your live webcast, at least until you understand the resources required.

When Should I Produce for On-Demand Delivery?

Of course, this whole book is built on the principle of on-demand. One of the great advantages of the Internet is instant access at any time to untold amounts of information, including video and audio information. But let's step back for a minute and consider the reasons for on-demand delivery of streams over live broadcasts.

You should consider producing for on-demand delivery when the content stays relatively fresh over time. Some people called this kind of content "evergreen," because it reminds them of the pine and fir trees that retain their green color over the darkest winter, unlike their deciduous cousins. Another factor that argues for on-demand is audience interest. Will the potential audience want to watch this content long after it was first produced? If the answer is yes, you should produce and store an on-demand streaming media file.

Some streams may fall into both live and on-demand categories. A live broadcast of a presidential speech is usually archived, because his words carry interest both at the time they were delivered and for many days, perhaps years afterward. Some good candidates for on-demand production and/or archiving include

- A training presentation on sexual harassment (This could be delivered live and archived for later access.)
- An early audio recording of the community's first radio station
- Almost any kind of music production

One major advantage of on-demand delivery over live delivery is your ability to enhance the stream with interactive elements. For example, you can apply some advanced techniques to add a navigation menu to a stream, allowing users to go to specific sections of a recording. This isn't possible in a live broadcast.

To help you make a decision on live vs. on-demand (or both), see the suggested decision matrix in Table 4.1.

Table 4.1. An On-Demand vs. Live Webcast Decision Matrix

| | | Broadcast Choices | | | | |
| | | Live | | On-Demand | | Both | |
Criteria	Weight	Rating	Score	Rating	Score	Rating	Score
Uncertain outcome							
Dramatic tension							
Info stays same over time							
Potential for interactivity							
Budget							
Potential to promote stream							
Prep time							
Totals							

Instructions for using this decision matrix:

1. Give each criterion a weight from 1 (not important) to 10 (very important).
2. Rate how well each platform meets the criterion.
3. Multiply the weight by the rating for a score.
4. Add the score for each platform. The highest score suggests the right decision.

Streaming Protocols

All data needs to be organized in a certain way to make sense. Books have chapters, sections, and paragraphs. The rules of grammar in a human language let two or more people communicate, because they agree on the rules. Computer data have a kind of "grammar" as well. When computers talk to each other across a network, they use a "communications protocol" or just "protocol."

Computer programmers have come up with an alphabet soup of protocols. A few are directly related to streaming media. The protocols control the communications between the media player and the streaming server, and vice versa. Here's a list of the most important, plus a brief explanation of each:

User Datagram Protocol (UDP): UDP is one of the most common Internet protocols used for sending data in a continuous stream. It uses less error correction than another common Internet protocol, Transmission Control Protocol (TCP), meaning there are fewer transmission delays.

Real Time Streaming Protocol (RTSP): The RTSP protocol is an open standard application-level protocol endorsed by the Internet Engineering Task Force (IETF), a body of prominent Internet engineers. Internet clients, i.e., media players, use RTSP to talk to streaming servers, allowing features such as Play/Pause/Stop. If you look inside a RealNetworks or Apple QuickTime metafile, the first four letters are often "rtsp." That tells you the player will use RTSP to communicate with the streaming server. RTSP is supported by virtually all streaming media vendors.

Real Time Transport Protocol (RTP): Streaming media servers build packets of data and send them off to the media player. RTP (We're not sure what happened to the other "T.") governs how the server constructs these packets. For example, RTP lays out rules for identifying the type of packet, how packets are numbered in sequence, and how they are stamped with the date and time. The architecture is similar to UDP and TCP, though RTP packets are meant to work specifically with the RTSP and RTCP protocols.

Real Time Control Protocol (RTCP): RTCP packets work with RTP packets to check the delivery of other packets. RTCP packets are often used to monitor quality of service.

Progressive Networks Audio (PNA): RealNetworks was dubbed "Progressive Networks" by its founders, and its early engineers

Continued

developed a proprietary protocol called "PNA." It's rarely used these days.

Microsoft Media Services (MMS): Microsoft also developed a proprietary streaming protocol, MMS, which is widely used today on its Windows Media servers. RealNetworks supports MMS on later versions of its media player and server. If you open a Windows Media metafile, the first three letters of the streaming URL are usually "mms."

HyperText Transfer Protocol (HTTP): Most kinds of data we see on the Internet, particularly web pages, use HTTP. Every time you see an "http" in a web address, you know it's using HTTP as the communications protocol. In streaming, HTTP is most often used for "progressive downloading," sometimes called "pseudo-streaming," because it doesn't have the control and data management features of "true" streaming protocols, such as RTSP. Flash MX audio and video are usually placed on web servers, and the files are streamed under HTTP.

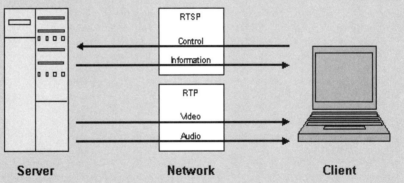

Server   **Network**   **Client**

Figure 4.1   How the RTSP and RTP protocols work together.

Get Ready to Serve Your Streams

When you approach your IT department or a web hosting company about serving your streams, we think you should have a grasp of the technology fundamentals and the infrastructure needs that go into streaming delivery. You'll find it easier to trust networking professionals if you know something of what they talk about. The basics are relatively easy to grasp, even you're not a techie. The next few sections will give you the background necessary for making good decisions in partnership with the pros. As the saying goes, forewarned is forearmed.

You may want to review "Choosing the Right Streaming Format: Evaluating Your Audience and Resources" in Chapter 3. Many of the issues, such as bandwidth, have counterparts on the delivery side of the equation.

Operating System and Streaming Server Considerations

Just as you evaluated the potential streaming media platforms of your audience (RealPlayer, Windows Media Player, QuickTime, Flash, or some combination thereof), you need to evaluate the platforms available to you on the server side. The server side of the platform is usually thought of in terms of the operating system, followed by the streaming server supported by the operating system.

There are two basic server operating system choices: Microsoft products, such as Windows NT and Windows Server 2003, or the family of systems that trace their roots to the original Unix operating system developed by Bell Labs in the 1970s. Unix-like systems include

- HP-UX (Hewlett Packard)
- Solaris (Sun Microsystems)
- AIX (IBM)
- BSD (open source)
- Linux (open source)

Once you know the operating system your network servers use (as opposed to desktop computers, which run either Microsoft Windows or Apple Computer's operating system), you'll know more about your streaming server options. That's because some streaming servers run on some operating systems and not others. Here's a general rundown:

- RealNetworks Helix: Runs on Windows servers and major Unix OSs
- Microsoft Windows Media Services: Runs on Windows server only
- QuickTime Streaming Server: Runs on Macintosh server only
- Macromedia Flash MX: Streamed by web servers, which run on virtually all operating systems

Furthermore, most streaming servers support more than one format. But format support is not equal among all streaming platforms. For example, RealNetworks Helix will stream almost any kind of audio or video file, including those of the company's arch rival, Microsoft. However, Bill Gates won't allow Microsoft Media Services to stream files created with RealNetworks' tools. Moreover, because the streaming landscape is constantly shifting, there's a chance (however slight) that Bill might change his mind, muddying the waters.

Confused? No? You must be a genius, because this stuff confuses and frustrates the heck outta us. Your only solution is to carefully study the system requirements and capabilities of all the streaming servers on the market and compare your findings to the capabilities in your shop. Then you can work with your system administrator to make the wisest choice.

Here's an example: Let's assume your network has no streaming capability at all. You want to stream QuickTime files. You learn from your IT priestess that your network runs on Microsoft Windows 2003 Server. That means she can install Windows Media Services or RealNetworks Helix Server. If the web server is working, you can also stream Flash MX. But you're out of luck if you want to install QuickTime Streaming Server. Ah, fudge! Not to worry. Helix can stream QuickTime files.

Security

Most of us have heard of computer viruses, malicious lines of code that invade our desktop computers and erase files and even erase hard drives. Criminal coders also attack servers, and streaming servers are no exception. But security issues in the streaming world go far beyond self-protection, and they can even be a handicap to delivery of your streams to the end-user.

Firewalls

A computer firewall takes its name from a barrier that protects something valuable from something dangerous on the other side. In an automobile, the firewall protects people from a catastrophic failure in the engine compartment. Computer firewalls typically limit the kinds of Internet data that can pass into and out of an internal network. Most network administrators think of the Internet as a dangerous wilderness full of virtual beasts that could attack at any time. For them, a firewall is like a castle wall with limited access points, allowing only certain kinds of information in or out.

Most firewalls are configured out of the box to reject streaming media. The nature of the back-and-forth communication between the media player and server, and the types of protocols and packets exchanged, are usually problematic to firewalls. People behind a firewall at government organizations and large corporations are the most frequent victims of firewall issues; system administrators are correctly trying to limit access in an effort to thwart invaders. However, with a little bit of persuasion and elbow grease, firewalls and "sysadmins" (a nickname for system administrators) can be trained to safely allow streaming media data.

Here are some methods of coping with firewalls:

HTTP cloaking: Most firewalls allow data packets that use the HTTP protocol, the protocol for web pages. If you are sending streams to others you think are behind a firewall, consider using "http cloaking," which wraps data packets in a kind of HTTP envelope. The packets may get past the firewall, though the user experience may not be as good as it would be without cloaking. But at least they're getting the audio or video.

Special server location: It's just unnatural for streaming media servers to live behind firewalls. They crave the freedom of the Internet, because they need to communicate back and forth with media players. If you run a streaming server, ask your network administrator to put it in a "demilitarized zone," or "DMZ." The term comes from international politics. Two warring nations, when they get tired of shooting at each other, agree to a buffer zone a few miles wide. No soldiers or weapons are allowed in the DMZ, and people feel safer. In computer networking, the DMZ is just outside the firewall facing the stormy, unpredictable Internet "cloud." You have control of the streaming server, and it can talk freely to end-users out in the wider world.

Education: You should prepare yourself to educate end-users, as well as network and system administrators, about configuring media players to work behind a firewall. Some networks may dedicate a "port," a kind of virtual window, through which streaming data travels. Or your network administrator may prefer to use a "proxy" server, which is a way to store Internet data for use by designated people. In each case, the media player's settings need to be modified.

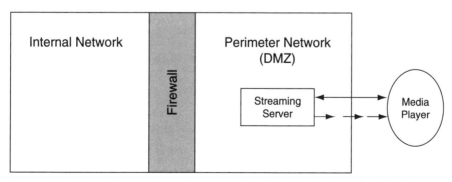

Figure 4.2 A typical network configuration with a "demilitarized zone," or DMZ.

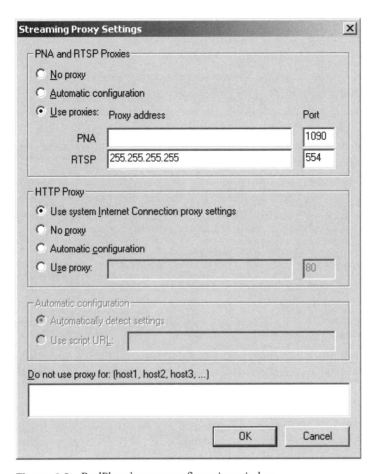

Figure 4.3   RealPlayer's proxy configuration window.

Proxy Servers and Streaming

A special server called a "proxy" is a security measure of choice for many network administrators. If you configure a media player to use a proxy server, you're asking it to ask the proxy server to get the information for you. It acts as a kind of go-between, so that you don't ever connect to the Internet directly. Governments and corporations use proxy servers to hide information about themselves from folks who aren't supposed to know, such as hackers. Proxies can also filter incoming information, hiding it from people behind the proxy.

Patching the Holes in Software

Most software has imperfections. Malicious programmers know this, and they relish the challenge of finding the problems and exploiting them. Software vendors release code "patches" to plug holes hackers and others discover. Your server administrator is responsible for keeping your organization's systems up-to-date. As a streaming producer, it's wise for you to keep an eye on the streaming vendors' websites for news about their products. When you see security warnings or patch announcements, notify your IT department.

Authentication

The major streaming software manufacturers include "authentication" features in their streaming systems. When implemented, the end-user is asked for a user-name and password in order to access a stream. You usually see authentication systems when producers want to limit access to special groups, such as sub-scribers. However, most people password-protect their content via the web server, rather than the streaming server.

Digital Rights Management

We mentioned "digital rights management" or "DRM" in Chapter 3 when we talked about encoding. Streaming media server vendors also sell DRM tools for the server side. Music producers and retailers in particular want a way to ensure that their copyrights are protected. DRM is important to you if you want to prevent piracy of your media. Typical DRM features include

- Strong encryption to prevent unauthorized use of content
- Producer-defined business rules for accessing content
- Content licensing verification ("Are you authorized to view this file?")
- License auditing to allow tracking of royalty payments
- Support for non-desktop computer devices, such as handheld devices

File Storage

Streaming media files take up a lot of room, even though they're highly compressed. If you plan to serve a large amount of video, you will need very large hard drives, perhaps even whole systems devoted to file storage and retrieval.

How much do you need? That depends on several factors, such as your encoding practices. Files encoded for dialup delivery need less space than files delivered exclusively over a corporate LAN. See Table 4.1 for some guidance.

Table 4.2. Streaming media file sizes

Target Bandwidth	Audio	Video
56 Kbps modem	0.24 Megabytes/minute	0.25 Megabytes/minute
112 Kbps dual ISDN	0.47 Megabytes/minute	0.59 Megabytes/minute
Corporate LAN	0.70 Megabytes/minute	1.10 Megabytes/minute
256 Kbps cable/DSL modem	0.70 Megabytes/minute	1.65 Megabytes/minute
512 Kbps cable/DSL modem	0.70 Megabytes/minute	3.30 Megabytes/minute

Use these per-minute figures to estimate the final sizes of encoded audio and video files. Multiply the length of the file in minutes by the number of megabytes per minute. If you use multiple bit rate encoding, add the figures for each type (audio or video) and bandwidth together. The figures in the table come from RealNetworks. But they should be more or less applicable to other vendors' codecs. Be conservative in your estimates.

Bandwidth

We've talked about bandwidth needs up to this point in the context of the end-user. (Are they connecting with dialup, cable/DSL, or by a corporate LAN?) The end-user needs only enough bandwidth to view one audio or video stream. When you serve streams to your internal audience or the outside world, you need to think about bandwidth in terms of the aggregate number of simultaneous connections to your streaming server. In other words, if 10 dialup users connect to your streaming server, you'll need at least 600 kilobytes per second of outgoing bandwidth. (10 × 56 kbps = 560 kbps + 40 kbps [headroom] = 600 kbps) You also have to take into account other activity on your network, such as email and web browsing. Where's this leading? You may have to add extra bandwidth capacity to your network, which may mean increased costs. Bandwidth is the single largest ongoing technical infrastructure expense in the streaming media delivery equation.

To understand this better, let's quickly review how the client and the server work together. You'll recall that the server sends continuous streams of data to the media player. Just like autos on an expressway need space to move smoothly and freely, data needs space in the form of bandwidth to travel. If too many autos try to reach the same destination, you get a traffic jam. If too much data tries to elbow its way through the bandwidth connection, data gets backed up, and you get a frustrating user experience.

> ### Video: Two Streams in One
>
> It's worth remembering that video streams are actually *two* streams, one for the sound and one for the pictures. For example, a 56K stream may reserve 8 kilobytes per second for audio, 26 kbps for video, and 22 kbps for "overhead," which is data that controls the delivery of the entire stream.

How much bandwidth do you need? Go back to your audience analysis in Chapter 3. Two main questions apply:

- What's your best estimate of the peak number of connections you expect at a given moment? Ten? Hundreds? Thousands? This number is usually discussed using the term "simultaneous connections" or "simultaneous streams."
- What streaming bit rates does your audience expect? Dialup only? Cable/DSL? Higher?

Use these two variables to calculate a rough estimate of the amount of bandwidth you need. For example, if you expect a peak of 100 simultaneous connections at 225 kbps (a common bit rate for cable/DSL connections), you'll need at least 2.25 megabytes of bandwidth. Double the minimum figure for safety. Let your network administrator know you need at least 4.5 megabytes per second of outgoing bandwidth. Ask for as much bandwidth as you can get. You'll never have enough.

Unicasting and Multicasting

The delivery of streams to media players almost always follows a simple model: one stream for each client connection. This is called "unicasting." It's the easiest model to grasp and implement, but it also uses the most bandwidth. What if you could get all your players to tap into a single stream? You'd need far less bandwidth. This is called "multicasting," which requires a specially configured network. Ask your IT guru if your network is multicast-enabled. If so, you may be able to add streaming capacity without drastically increasing your bandwidth consumption. It's unlikely, though, you'll be able to multicast to audiences outside your internal network. The public Internet isn't set up for it.

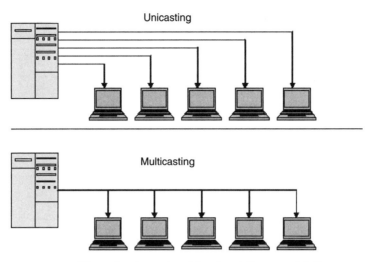

Figure 4.4   The unicasting and multicasting delivery models for streams.

Buying a Streaming Server

You've analyzed your audience and reviewed your organization's streaming capabilities, and you've decided you should purchase a streaming server. Do you really need one? Throughout this book, we've assumed you'll use server software specially designed to deliver audio and video over a computer network. That's usually the best option. However, especially if Macromedia Flash MX is your streaming technology of choice, you have another option, which won't cost you a dime.

HTTP Streaming

We make a distinction in this book between "true" streaming, which uses specialized streaming protocols, such as RTSP, and a second type, called by various names, including "pseudo-streaming," "progressive download," or "HTTP streaming." As the last name suggests, the second type of streaming uses the HTTP protocol. It's the same protocol web browsers use to communicate with web servers.

The principle is pretty simple: You treat your encoded file just like an HTML file or graphics file by putting it on your web server. You create a link to the encoded file in the same way you create a link to another web page. (See the Macromedia Flash example below.) The user clicks the link and the encoded media file starts to download. As it downloads, it starts the media player, which plays the file as it comes through. In many cases, the user experience with HTTP streaming is virtually the same as "true" streaming. But there are limits.

First, your system administrator will have to configure your web server to understand the MIME type associated with your type of encoded file. That's actually pretty easy. (See the box on MIME types in Chapter 1 in the section "Common Metafile Creation Steps." See also Table 4.3 for a list of common streaming MIME types.) Second, you'll probably run into performance problems with the stream after a certain amount of time. The longer a stream is, the more problems you'll experience, such as sudden stops.

Third, if large numbers of people request the stream all at once, your network could be easily swamped. Web servers, unlike streaming servers, typically don't know how to manage the bandwidth allocated to them. You also miss out on such features as multiple bit rate encoding, because web servers can't detect modem speed. Therefore, they don't know when to serve a high-bandwidth or low-bandwidth version of your stream.

HTTP streaming is a good option under the following circumstances:

- Macromedia Flash MX is your media player of choice. (HTTP streaming works with other media players, too.)
- Your audio/video files are less than 60 seconds in length.
- You expect a minimal number of simultaneous requests.
- You encode with only one bit rate.
- You need on-demand access only. (Web servers can't serve live streams.)

Table 4.3. Common MIME Types for Encoded Streaming Files

Vendor	File Extension	MIME Type
RealNetworks	`.ra, .rv, .rm`	audio/x-pn-realaudio
Microsoft	`.asf, .wma, .wmv`	video/x-ms-asf
Apple Computer	`.mov`	video/quicktime
Macromedia	`.swf`	application/x-shockwave-flash

Add these MIME types to your web server configuration if you use HTTP streaming. Note that other MIME types exist for these file types. Check the online documentation for each streaming vendor for a complete list.

The Advantages of "True" Streaming

As we mentioned above, "true" streaming relies on specialized network transport protocols, such as RTSP, which are supported by streaming servers, not web servers. The protocols allow the client and server to speak to each other and adjust to "net weather," the dynamic network conditions that pervade the Internet and even some internal networks. The final result is better network performance, more efficient use of resources, and a higher quality user experience. Use a streaming server under the following circumstances:

- Your encoded files are more than 60 seconds long.
- You expect more than a minimal amount of simultaneous connections.

- You plan multiple bit rate encoding.
- You may stream live events sometime in the future.
- You want consistent performance for long files.
- You need intelligent management of your outgoing bandwidth.

Licensing

The main drawback of specialized streaming servers is cost. You have to buy the server, or more accurately, the privilege of using the server. Remember when you installed your media players and encoders in Chapter 1? Part of the installation process included a screen that asked you to accept or reject a bunch of legalese. If you rejected it, the software wouldn't install. When you accepted it, you in effect said that you agree to abide by the conditions of a license offered by the manufacturer. Even though the software is installed on your hard drive, you don't really own the software, just the right to use it in a way defined by the manufacturer.

The same goes for streaming servers. However, different manufacturers license their servers in different ways. Here's a breakdown of the different licensing approaches:

- *RealNetworks:* RealNetworks licenses its streaming server based primarily on the number of simultaneous connections you expect to serve at one time. Licensing starts with a free version, which limits you to 1 megabyte per second of throughput. That could work out to 15 or so 56K streams or just two 500K streams. From here, pricing starts in the low four figures. RealNetworks' serving license pricing changes fairly frequently. Check the website for the latest.
- *Microsoft:* The Redmond, Washington, behemoth's Windows Media Services comes "free" with its enterprise server products. Of course, you have to buy the server products, which are sold based on the number of users. Costs for enterprise servers can run from several hundred dollars to darn near infinity, depending on your overall networking needs. However, if your network already runs on Microsoft products, you can install Windows Media Services without spending more money.
- *Apple Computer:* Apple's QuickTime Streaming Server has the simplest licensing arrangement. You buy a license for the server itself; licensing is not related to the number of streams you serve. In fact, Apple touts this as a feature, jibing its competition for what Apple calls a "server tax," that is, charging more money for streaming licenses as streaming volume increases.
- *Macromedia:* Macromedia sells a server with streaming capacity, but most Flash MX developers stream their work from web servers. We recommend you do the same with your Flash MX until you have a stronger grasp of streaming technology.

Open Source Licensing

You may have heard of another class of software licensing called "open source." The price for an open source license is pretty compelling: $0. Chapter 5 will look at open source streaming solutions in some detail. But it's worth noting here that Apple has released an open source version of its QuickTime Streaming Server. Called "Darwin Streaming Server," it follows the open source licensing model.

Technical Support

What do you do if the server's not working and the manual is no help? The answer is often technical support provided by the manufacturer. The purchase of a server license usually includes some level of technical support, ranging from an online archive of accumulated experience (a "knowledge base") to a dedicated human being 24 × 7 × 365. One factoid: If you think you're talking to a support person in Anytown, USA, you may in fact be talking to someone in Anytown, India. American software manufacturers of all types are outsourcing more and more help-related services overseas.

There are a few other options. When an error message pops up or something else breaks, there's a very good chance that someone else has experienced the same problem. You might find a local user's group that has an online bulletin board where you can post questions. Several websites cater to techno-geeks, and they include message board areas. The vendors themselves run message boards. We've solved several technical problems by performing a global web search or a search of online news groups using the text of an error message. The Internet is an unparalleled collection of human wisdom and folly on the subject of computers.

Advanced Metafiles

You'll recall from Chapter 1 that the divided functions of web server and streaming media server require the use of a "metafile." (See the "Prepare to Create a Metafile" section in Chapter 1 and following, especially "Common Metafile Creation Steps.") To quickly review, a streaming media metafile is a small text file on your web server that contains an URL pointing a media player to the location of the streaming media file on your streaming server. We won't repeat all the background stuff in Chapter 1, but here's a quick review of what happens:

1. User clicks a link to the metafile.
2. The browser downloads the metafile.

3. The browser hands the metafile to the media player.
4. The media player looks inside the metafile for the URL to the streaming media file.
5. The media player contacts the streaming media server and plays the file.

Metafiles can do more than just point to the streaming server. They can control several features in the player. You can override some data encoded into a file with new information, such as the copyright information. An ambitious programmer can build dozens or hundreds of new metafiles instantly whenever he or she chooses, with only a small amount of scripted code. Or you can even create metafiles "on the fly," using information from a database. We'll go through each vendor's main metafile features to show you your options.

More on Metafiles

Every metafile has at least an URL to a streaming file. Each piece of the URL has a meaning. Here's a typical URL:
mms://streams.yourhost.com:1755/pathtofile/filename.wmv
Another way to look at a streaming URL is
[protocol]://[your.domain]:[port]/[mount_point]/[path]/[file.name]
Let's take the URL apart, piece by piece.

Protocol: This is the streaming protocol used by the server. In our example, it's Microsoft Media Services protocol. Note the colon and pair of forward slashes that follow the protocol.

Domain: This is the familiar string of characters ending in .com. Note the optional colon that follows the domain name.

Port: The number in our example, 1755, identifies the requested service to the computer where the service lives, in this case, Windows Media Services. The RTSP protocol uses port 554. Port numbers are usually optional.

Mount point: The mount point is the beginning place in the streaming media server's file system or directory structure where streaming files are located. The mount point is set in the server's configuration files.

Path: The directory or directories under the mount point where a specific file is located. A file could be located directly under the mount point.

File name: The name of the file to stream. In our example, the .wmv extension signals it's a Windows Media file.

RealNetworks Metafile (`.ram`, `.rpm`) *Options*

You put options on the end of an URL to a RealNetworks streaming server that start and end at a specific time and/or modify title, author, and copyright information. The URL is contained within a text file with the extension `.ram`. The extension is `.rpm` if you're using the embedded player. (See the section "Set Up Your Web Page" below.) Here's the format:

rtsp://streams.helixserver.com/filename.rm?[parameter]=[value]&[parameter]=[value]

Note the "?" after the filename and the "&" between the first and second pairs of parameters and values.

Here's a simple URL with options pointing to a RealNetworks Helix Server: rtsp://streams.helixserver.com/filename.rm?start="30"&end="1:45"

This tells the server to send data starting from this file at the 30-second mark and stopping at the 1-minute-45-second mark. See Table 4.4 for common RealNetworks metafile parameters.

Table 4.4. Common metafile parameters for RealNetworks' metafiles

Parameter	Values	Purpose
start	dd = days hh = hours mm = minutes ss = seconds xyz = milliseconds Written as dd:hh:mm:ss.xyz	Sets a start time within a file
end	dd = days hh = hours mm = minutes ss = seconds xyz = milliseconds Written as dd:hh:mm:ss.xyz	Sets an end time within a file
title	Any string of characters	Overrides title info encoded in the file
author	Any string of characters	Overrides author info encoded in the file
copyright	Any string of characters	Overrides copyright info encoded in the file

Windows Media Metafile (`.asx`) *Options*

Windows Media metafiles have a completely different structure from RealNetworks' metafiles. They use an XML-like syntax, which resembles HTML syntax, but is more flexible and precise. Here are the contents of a simple Windows Media metafile, which has the extension `.asx`:

```
<asx version="3.0">
    <entry>
        <starttime value="30"/>
        <duration value="1:15"/>
        <title>My New Title</title>
        <ref href= "mms://streams.wmserver.com/filename.wmv"/>
    </entry>
</asx>
```

This metafile tells a Windows Media server to play the file starting at 30 seconds from the beginning and run it for 1 minute 15 seconds. The file will stop playing at the 1-minute-45-second mark. The file also changes the title encoded into the streaming file to "My New Title." Carefully note the syntax of each line, down to the slashes, which are easy to miss.

Also note the difference between the **starttime** tag and the **title** tag. **Starttime** and **duration** take a `value`, in this case, the time in seconds to start the file and the amount of time to play the file. **Title** is a "container" tag. It doesn't take a value, but wraps around some information with a closing tag. See Table 4.5 for common Windows Media metafile options.

Table 4.5. Common Windows Media metafile options

Parameter	Options	Purpose
<asx version="3.0"> </asx>	n/a	Encloses entire metafile
<entry> </entry>	n/a	Encloses clip information
<ref href="mms://xxx"/>	n/a	Specifies an URL to streaming file
<starttime value="x"/>	dd = days hh = hours mm = minutes ss = seconds Written as dd:hh:mm:ss	Sets a start time within a file
<duration value="x"/>	dd = days hh = hours mm = minutes ss = seconds Written as dd:hh:mm:ss	Sets a duration for playback
<title> </title>	Any string of characters	Overrides title information encoded in the file
<author> </author>	Any string of characters	Overrides author information encoded in the file
<copyright> </copyright>	Any string of characters	Overrides copyright information encoded in the file

QuickTime (.`qtl`) Metafiles

The QuickTime metafile has the extension .`qtl`. But before doing anything, contact your system administrator and ask him or her to add the MIME type **application/x-quicktimeplayer** to the web server's configuration files. Unlike .`ram` and .`asx`, .`qtl` is not a common file extension. Now for some good news for people who don't like to code. Apple's QuickTime Pro 6 has a graphical tool for creating metafiles. All you have to do is fill in the blanks. Here's the procedure:

1. Start QuickTime Pro 6.
2. Select Open Movie in New Player and select your encoded file.
3. From the File menu, select Export.
4. Find your encoded QuickTime file and select it.
5. In the Export drop-down menu, select "Movie to QuickTime Media Link." Note that the file now has the .`qtl` extension. If not, change the file extension to .`qtl` to avoid overwriting your encoded media file.
6. Click the Options button to open the QuickTime Media Link Settings dialog box.
7. In the URL field, type the URL to your file on your streaming server.
8. Leave the Type field blank.
9. Enter a title for your movie in the Name field.
10. Click OK.
11. Click Save.

You can look at the innards of a simple .`qtl` file by opening it with a text editor, such as Notepad:

```
<?xml version="1.0"?>
<?quicktime type="application/x-quicktime-media-link"?>
<embed moviename="My Title" src="rtsp://www.myqtserver.com/myfile.mov"/>
```

XML and XML Compliant

Observant readers noted the **xml** in the QuickTime metafile code. XML (eXtensible Markup Language) is the current darling of the programming world. It's an extremely flexible way to describe data within a document. You don't need to know XML to create streaming media, but it's worth learning about. You may have also noted that the Windows Media metafile code looks a little like the QuickTime code. That's because the Windows Media code is "XML compliant," meaning it follows standard XML syntax.

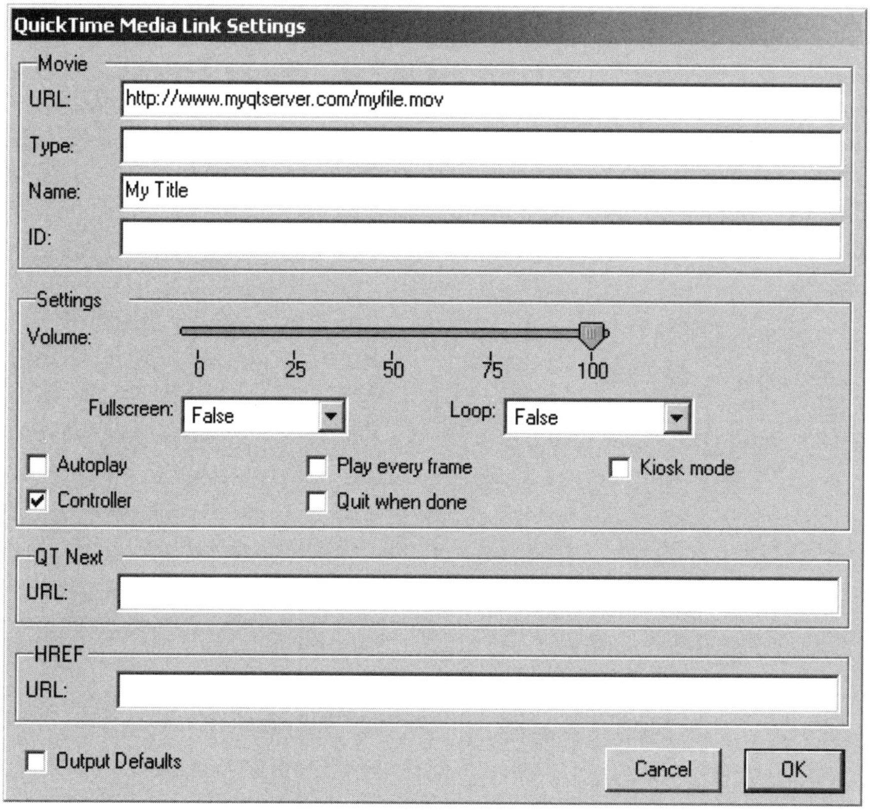

Figure 4.5   The QuickTime Media Link Settings dialog box.

No Metafiles for Flash

Macromedia Flash MX does not use metafiles, since they are usually served from a web server. See the next section for information on using Flash MX files in your web page.

Dynamically Generated Metafiles

RealNetworks Helix Server offers an easy way to skip all this metafile rigmarole. The server will generate a metafile "on the fly," that is, it creates the metafile when you need it. You don't have to worry about building it and uploading it to the web server. To generate a metafile dynamically, create a hypertext reference (HREF) directly to the streaming server. The HTML link will look something like this:

<a href="http://streams.helixserver.com: 80/ramgen/video_file.rm">

Note the path "ramgen" in the URL. This tells the Helix server to build the `.ram` file automatically and send it to the browser. The browser then sends the `.ram` file to the media player, which opens it, and locates the video file.

Later versions of RealServer, including Helix, also contain a way to generate an `.asx` metafile on the fly for Windows Media Players. In this case, the HTML code would use this syntax:

<a href="http://streams.helixserver. com:80/asxgen/video_file.wmv">

Check your Helix server documentation for exact use of the ramgen and asxgen features.

Windows Media Services and QuickTime Streaming Server do not have a similar feature. However, you can write Active Server Page (ASP) code that can do similar things for Windows Media Server. Check the tutorial at http://www.streamingmedia.com/tutorials/ view.asp?tutorial_id=105

Upload Your Metafile

Upload your completed metafile to your web server. Note the path, which you'll need to put in your web page containing the streaming link.

Set Up Your Web Page

We're going to suspend our discussion of the server side of streaming for a moment to return to the client side. Your audience will access your streaming media file primarily through a web page. We're going to talk about this here because the web page you create will go on your web server.

Putting streaming media in a web page is more complicated than most types of web content, and it's potentially the most confusing. That's because streaming media requires the use of a "helper" application, a piece of software that's not part of the web browser. In the case of streaming media, the helper application is the media player. The media player can be used in two ways: as a stand-alone application, or as a browser "plug-in." Each has advantages and disadvantages and different implementations. We'll go through each, step-by-step, and show you some code examples.

For purposes of clarity and brevity, we'll assume you're using a video file, not an audio-only file. Of course, you can use the code discussed below for audio-only applications as well.

External vs. Embedded Players

A web developer can take advantage of a media player's capabilities in two ways. First, he or she can tell the browser to play the stream in an external player. This is usually a stand alone application, that is, RealPlayer, Windows Media Player, or QuickTime Player. (The Flash Player works only within a browser.) When a user clicks a streaming link, the browser tells the media player to start up and play the file.

The developer can also tell the browser to play the media file within the browser window. In this case, the player is being used as an "embedded" application. When the player is installed, certain components become part of a browser "plug-in." These are a bit like the attachments to your vacuum cleaner. When you need to reach into a tight spot, you attach the crevasse tool to the hose. The tool becomes part of the vacuum cleaner for a short time. When a developer wants to play a streaming media file in a browser window, he or she adds some HTML that tells the browser to attach the streaming media components and play the file in the browser. When the user goes to a different page, the plug-in components are unloaded from the browser.

Should I Use the External Player or an Embedded Player?

Each form of the media player, external and embedded, has advantages and disadvantages. Web page coding for the external, stand-alone player is easiest. All you need to do is point to a metafile using a standard HTML hypertext reference ("HREF") tag. However, some users might be confused when the stand-alone player starts up on their computer. Also, the media player has it own logo and branding messages from the vendors, which may compete with your own, especially if you're targeting a consumer audience. As always, consult your audience analysis and communications goals for guidance.

If you use an embedded player, you have almost total control over the look and feel of the media player in the user's browser. You decide where to put the video image and the Play/Pause/Stop buttons, and you even determine what the buttons look like. However, it's harder to code HTML for embedded players. You'll need some advanced HTML knowledge and some knowledge of how different browsers behave. For really advanced control, you'll need to know some javascript or ActiveX coding.

HTML Coding for External Players

HTML code for stand-alone media players is very simple. All you need is an HREF tag within your web page. It works essentially the same for all players, except Flash, which doesn't use an external application.

<ahref="http://www.yourcompany.com/pathtometafile/mymetafile.XXX">My Audio/Video</a>

Replace the "XXX" with the correct file extension for your metafile, such as `.asx`.

HTML Coding for Embedded Players

HTML code for embedded players differs significantly from player to player, although they share several components. Most importantly, they all use the **<object>** and **<embed>** tags. Here's another confusing bit:

- **<object>** tags are used by Microsoft Internet Explorer to embed plug-ins.
- **<embed>** tags are used by Netscape Navigator to embed plug-ins.

Because you may not know which browser will display the page containing the code, you need to create "cross-platform" HTML. To do this, simply enclose your **<embed>** tags within **<object>** tags. The following code examples for each media player demonstrate this practice.

A ClassID by Itself

You'll note that the **<object>** tags for each of the following examples use a parameter called "classid" following by a seemingly random string of letters and numbers. It's important that you use the string *exactly as shown*. That code is needed by Internet Explorer to know how to load the ActiveX control associated with Windows Media Player. To learn more about ActiveX and classes, read the documentation on Microsoft's website. Several good how-to books on ActiveX are also available.

HTML for the RealPlayer Plug-In

Use this code for embedding RealPlayer components in a web page. We'll discuss each piece after the corresponding line of code. It's important to note that many of the components are used twice in RealPlayer. The first set of components controls the video image; the second set controls the Play/Pause/Stop buttons.

```
<OBJECT ID="video_image" CLASSID="clsid:CFCDAA03-8BE4-11cf-
B84B-0020AFBBCCFA" WIDTH="320" HEIGHT="240">
```

This line opens the **object** container, names the object in memory (important for javascript coding, if you elect to do so), sets the ActiveX control **classid,** and sets the **height** and **width** of the video image. The **height** and **width** should match the image size of the encoded file.

```
<PARAM NAME="AUTOSTART" VALUE="true">
```

The **autostart** parameter tells the player plug-in to play the video file when the web page loads. If you don't want the behavior, set the value to "false" or omit the parameter.

<PARAM NAME="TYPE" VALUE="audio/x-pn-realaudio">

The **type** parameter identifies the MIME type of the file to the browser.

<PARAM NAME="SRC" VALUE="my_video.rpm">

The **src** (short for "source") parameter points to the video's metafile. Note that RealPlayer uses the `.rpm` extension to identify a metafile used in the plug-in version of its player.

<PARAM NAME="CONTROLS" VALUE="ImageWindow">

The **controls** parameter tells the browser to use the video window component.

<PARAM NAME="CONSOLE" VALUE="_master">

The **console** parameter ties the "ImageWindow" controls parameter to the "ControlPanel" controls parameter below.

<EMBED NAME="video_image" SRC="my_video.rpm" WIDTH="320" HEIGHT="240" AUTOSTART="true" CONTROLS="ImageWindow" TYPE="audio/x-pn-realaudio-plugin" CONSOLE="_master">

The above is the opening **embed** tag for Netscape browsers. You can see the corresponding parameters. However, Netscape Navigator does not have a parameter corresponding to Internet Explorer's **classid**.

</EMBED>

The closing tag for the **embed** container.

</OBJECT>

The closing tag for the **object** container.

<OBJECT ID="video_controls" CLASSID="clsid:CFCDAA03-8BE4-11cf-B84B-0020AFBBCCFA" HEIGHT="36" WIDTH="320">

The opening **object** tag for the player controls. Note the different value for **id** and the smaller **height** value compared to the first set of tags.

<PARAM NAME="AUTOSTART" VALUE="true">

<PARAM NAME="TYPE" VALUE="audio/x-pn-realaudio">

<PARAM NAME="SRC" VALUE="my_video.rpm">

<PARAM NAME="CONTROLS" VALUE="ControlPanel">

This value for **controls** tells the browser to load the Play/Pause/Stop components.

<PARAM NAME="CONSOLE" VALUE="_master">

```
<EMBED NAME="video_controls" SRC="my_video.rpm" WIDTH="320"
HEIGHT="36" AUTOSTART="true" CONTROLS="ControlPanel"
TYPE="audio/x-pn-realaudio-plugin" CONSOLE="_master">

</EMBED>

</OBJECT>
```

HTML for the Windows Media Player Plug-In

Use this code for embedding Windows Media Player components in a web page. You can change some of the values for parameters, such as **height** and **width,** to suit your own needs.

```
<OBJECT ID="MMPlayer1" WIDTH="320" HEIGHT="350"
CLASSID="clsid:22d6f312-b0f6-11d0-94ab-0080c74c7e95"
TYPE="application/x-oleobject">
```

The opening **object** tag includes **id,** which is a name in memory for the player object. **Width** and **height** parameters correspond to the video image size *plus* the height of the player controls. The MIME **type** is also included in the opening **object** tag.

```
<PARAM NAME="FileName" VALUE="my_video.asx">
```

The **FileName** parameter tells the plug-in where to find the metafile. You may need to add more path information to this value.

```
<PARAM NAME="ShowControls" VALUE="1">
```

The **ShowControls** parameter tells the browser to show the Play/Pause/Stop controls.

```
<PARAM NAME="AutoStart" VALUE="1">
```

The **autostart** parameter tells the browser whether or not to start the video when the page loads. In this case, the value of "1" means "Yes." A value of "0" means "No."

```
<EMBED NAME="MMPlayer1" TYPE="application/x-mplayer2"
SRC="my_video.asx" AUTOSTART="1" SHOWCONTROLS="1"
WIDTH="320" HEIGHT="350">
```

The opening **embed** tag for Netscape Navigator.

```
</EMBED>

</OBJECT>
```

HTML for the QuickTime Player Plug-In

The following HTML code will embed QuickTime Player plug-in components in a web page.

<OBJECT MOVIENAME="my_video" CLASSID="clsid:02BF25D5-8C17-4B23-BC80-D3488ABDDC6B" HEIGHT="350" WIDTH="240">

The opening **object** tag for QuickTime Players. Note the **moviename** parameter, which is used in place of the **id** parameter for other players.

<PARAM NAME="TYPE" VALUE="video/quicktime">

The **type** parameter identifies the MIME type to the browser.

<PARAM NAME="SRC" VALUE="my_video.qtl">

The **src** parameter tells the plug-in where the metafile is located on the web server.

<PARAM NAME="AUTOPLAY" VALUE="true">

An **autoplay** parameter set to "true" will start the video immediately after the web page loads. The default value is "false."

<PARAM NAME="CONTROLLER" VALUE="true">

The **controller** parameter shows the Play/Pause/Stop buttons.

<EMBED NAME="my_video" SRC="my_video.qtl" TYPE="video/quicktime" WIDTH="350" HEIGHT="240" AUTOPLAY="true" CONTROLLER="true">

These are the **embed** tag parameters for Netscape Navigator compatibility.

</EMBED>

</OBJECT>

HTML for the Flash MX Player Plug-In

This HTML embeds the Flash media player in your web page. Note that the Flash MX application you used to create the `.swf` file will also generate embedding HTML for you. You do this at the time you use the "Publish" command. See the section on Flash encoding in Chapter 3.

<OBJECT ID="my_video" CLASSID="clsid:D27CDB6E-AE6D-11cf-96B8-444553540000" WIDTH="320" HEIGHT="240">

The opening **object** tag for Flash.

<PARAM NAME="TYPE" VALUE="application/x-shockwave-flash">

The MIME **type** for Flash MX.

<PARAM NAME="movie" VALUE="my_video.swf">

The **movie** parameter points directly to the `.swf` video file, rather than a metafile for other players. That's because we stream Flash files off the web server, not a streaming media server.

```
<EMBED NAME="my_video" SRC="my_video.swf" WIDTH="320"
HEIGHT="240" TYPE="application/x-shockwave-flash">
```

The opening **embed** container tag for cross-platform compatibility with Netscape Navigator. The **src** parameter corresponds to the **movie** parameter in the **object** tag.

```
</EMBED>
```

```
</OBJECT>
```

Sorry, No Guarantees

It's unfortunate, but we can't guarantee the above code will automatically work for you. There are enough differences among player versions and browser versions to make universally compatible code almost impossible. This is the bane of all web developers and it causes sleepless nights. Maybe someday all the media player and browser vendors will agree to use standard tags, parameters, values, etc. In the meantime, you'll have to experiment some and test rigorously.

Upload Your Web Page

When you have completed your HTML coding, upload the file to your web server. You'll probably use your FTP program to do this. Note the location of the web page. You'll need it to test and announce your work.

Testing

Every software project includes a testing phase. Yours is no different. Depending on the complexity of your project, you should consider writing a test plan. Software engineers spend weeks writing test plans, which can run dozens of pages long. Yours could be as simple as a single page. The first thing to do is go back to your audience analysis from Chapter 3. Try to test on all the variables you expect to encounter. Test variables could include

- Operating systems
- Browsers and web pages, including the streaming links
- Media player(s)
- Player performance
- End-user bandwidth (dialup, cable/DSL, etc.)
- Server-side bandwidth usage

A tutorial on testing is beyond the scope of this book. But if you try to emulate as many of the technical conditions of your audience as best you can, you'll be more confident that your streaming project will perform as designed. Get your systems and network administrators involved. They will help you set up tests and troubleshoot problems.

Promote Your Streams

It sometimes amazes us that people sweat blood to make a killer streaming project, but don't bother to tell anybody about it! You've worked dang hard. Tell the world! Again, keep your audience in mind. Targeted announcements work best. Some of your options include

- An email with a link directly to the stream or to a web page with instructions
- Notices on all relevant web pages on your intranet
- Banner advertising on websites your audience visits
- An announcement on a printed postcard sent via snail mail
- Standing on a corner and shouting at the top of your lungs (well, maybe not)

The important thing is relevance. Where do you think the audience is most likely to see an announcement about your stream? You might ask someone with public relations or advertising/marketing experience for advice. They can help your investment pay off by finding ways to maximize your exposure in a productive way.

Outsourcing to a Streaming Media Hosting Service

Many, if not the majority, of small to medium-sized businesses contract with a hosting company to host their web site. The company handles all the files and processes that make a site work, such as HTML files, databases, and programs that make the site dynamic. Even home Internet service accounts have a little bit of web storage space for personal home pages.

Many hosting companies and Internet Service Providers (ISPs) also offer streaming media services. Web hosting has evolved a standard set of options, such as web serving, email accounts, and credit card order processing. However, streaming services vary wildly from one hosting company to another. Some offer none. Others offer everything. Furthermore, a few companies have sprung up devoted exclusively to streaming media hosting and delivery. The industry of streaming media hosting is something of a wilderness at the moment. But it has definite staying power, given the background trends.

Is outsourcing streaming media hosting a good option for you? Review your audience analysis and your assessment of internal resources. If the two seem out of balance, and it seems impractical in terms of time and/or money to bring them into balance by adding internal capacity, outsourcing streaming media hosting and delivery is a viable option.

What Hosting Companies Can Do for You

The most important benefit of a hosting contract is peace of mind. You'll sleep better at night because the hosting company is taking care of important variables that could make or break the success of your streaming project. This is especially true if you plan to stream audio or video to a consumer audience. All you have to do is supply the content.

Hosting companies offer another important advantage: cost control. If you contract out your hosting, you don't have to spend the money to upgrade your network and systems infrastructure. Your upgrade could be as simple as adding streaming services to your current web hosting arrangement. Your monthly or quarterly charge goes up by a few percentage points, and you get all the streaming capacity you need. Because you pay a set amount per month or quarter, your streaming costs are more predictable, and budgeting is easier.

If you prefer to go with a streaming media hosting specialist, expect to purchase an account based on key streaming variables, notably storage space for files and the amount of data transferred per month, which is another way of talking about bandwidth. The more you need, the higher the cost, though economies of scale play a role in lowering unit costs. In addition, streaming specialists may offer encoding services, priced on a per-minute basis. The longer an audio or video program, the more you pay. But the process becomes much easier and simpler for you, the customer. You drop off a Beta SP or DV tape; they encode it, host it, and deliver it.

Other advantages of outsourcing include

- Security—Hosting companies make security a top priority, or they're out of business.
- Dedicated infrastructure—Streaming specialists and some web hosting companies optimize their networks for the unique demands of streaming.
- Advanced technology—Hosting companies have to keep up with the latest technological developments, or they risk falling behind competitors. This means you don't have to worry about buying the latest and greatest versions of everything every year or so.

Reasons to Avoid Outsourcing

The main thing you give up when you outsource is control. You are handing over an important part of your communications strategy, as well as tangible assets in the form of media files, to others. Granted, a hosting company has a compelling interest in providing good service and helping you succeed. But ultimately, you have the responsibility to ensure they can deliver your streams to your audience in a way that meets your goals. As President Ronald Reagan once said, "Trust, but verify." Keep your hosting provider up-to-date on your needs and expectations, and monitor its performance.

How to Shop for Streaming Media Hosting

You should shop for streaming media hosting just like anything else. Review your audience analysis and develop some criteria for deciding whether a hosting provider can meet your needs. Then call around. These questions will get you started:

1. What is your range of your services? End-to-end? Encoding only? Hosting only?
2. What streaming media platforms do you support?
3. What is your streaming media infrastructure? Do you have redundant backup systems?
4. How often do you upgrade your streaming servers? What is your standard server version for each platform you support?
5. Do you offer any uptime (service availability) guarantees?
6. What production facilities do you have? Do you offer live encoding at remote locations?
7. How much streaming experience do you have?
8. Can you show me a client list and references?
9. Can you report streaming media traffic?

Table 4.6. Common Pricing for Streaming Media Services

Encoding per format per bit rate

Media length	Rate per minute
0 to 30 minutes	$5.00 – $10.00
30 to 60 minutes	$2.50 – $7.50
More than 60 minutes	$1.00 – $3.50
Media storage	
Total amount	Rate per megabyte
Up to 1 gigabyte	$.05 – $.10
Up to 500 gigabytes	$.03 – $.07
Up to 1,000 gigabytes	$.01 – $.07
Data transfer	
Total amount	Rate per gigabyte
Up to 1 gigabyte	$10.00 – $15.00
Up to 500 gigabytes	$4.50 – $7.50
Up to 1,000 gigabytes	$3.00 – $7.00

Here's a sample of monthly prices for selected streaming media encoding and hosting components offered by streaming media specialists. *Caveat emptor.* Use this table for your own rough guesswork only. Actual pricing formulas vary wildly among providers. You should also expect to pay setup charges for some or all of these services.

10. Can you create customized web pages or embedded players?
11. Can you support advertising features, such as streaming ad insertion or banner ads?
12. What kind of customer support do you offer?

Chapter Summary

Chapter 4 showed you the factors that go into broadcasting your streaming media files. We started with a comparison of live streaming and on-demand streaming. Then we listed the infrastructure considerations that go into developing the capacity to serve streaming media to an internal and external audience. We showed you how to write streaming media metafiles, and how to add streaming media links to your web pages. Finally, we discussed your outsourcing options. In the next chapter, we'll look at alternative streaming media solutions and other advanced topics.

Live Broadcasting on the Internet Using Streaming Media

By Dan Rayburn

Recording and storing audio and video files is only one of the ways you can offer streaming media to an audience. Live streaming, sometimes called "webcasting," is the process of putting your audio and video online as it happens, that is, in "real time."

Live Internet broadcasting requires more resources than simply recording and archiving content for on-demand playback. Many times, the nature of the content calls for live broadcast, such as breaking news, a corporate announcement, or an investor relations call. However, if the content is not time-sensitive, you may want to allocate resources and budget needed for a live broadcast to other options, such as making the content available on-demand at a specified time and date.

Live webcasts also entail a different set of workflow issues, and the technical resources chosen will be the biggest factor in the event cost and complexity.

Let's use a Tiger Woods webcast produced for the American Express website as an example. One of streaming media's advantages is the ability to deliver a message across all geographical boundaries. American Express used streaming media to drive users to its U.S.-based website to see live golf tips from Tiger Woods. This exclusive, web-only broadcast let users interact with Woods and ask questions about their golf game.

Continued

At the same time, they could apply for American Express credit cards. Streaming media allowed the company to market to select individuals in hopes of getting them to sign up for the company's services.

A live event such as Tiger Woods offering golf tips is broken down into three main components: audio and/or video capture, content encoding, and delivery or distribution.

Audio and/or Video Capture

The first piece of any live event is content. Some events have just an audio component, such as a quarterly investor relations call. Others consist of video and audio. The first step in any live event is recording the content and capturing it for streaming. There are many ways to do this. The signal can be captured and encoded at the venue itself. You can capture the signal via a phone bridge, if the event is audio-only, such as a conference call. For remote events, an audio and video signal can be sent to a satellite ("uplinking") and pulled down (otherwise known as "downlinking") at another location. For American Express, the video was shot at the 18th hole of a London golf course and then fed into a satellite truck, where it was uplinked.

Content Encoding

After the Tiger Woods signal had been downlinked in New York, it needed to be encoded. Encoding is done by an "encoder," a computer with hardware and software that digitizes the signal into a streaming media format. For the Woods event, an audio-only feed was encoded for dialup users and a video feed was encoded for broadband users, both in the Windows Media format.

Delivery or Distribution

The content is now ready for delivery, also called "distribution." The encoded signal is sent via the Internet or a private connection to streaming servers sitting on a delivery network. The servers transmit the content to viewers. For most live events, Internet distribution is the largest cost because it requires you to have an infrastructure capable of handling traffic surges. Even companies that do some webcasting production in-house typically outsource delivery of the event to a Content Delivery Network (CDN), a service provider that specializes in Internet content distribution. For Tiger Woods, the live signal was sent to CDN servers in the U.S. and Europe. The CDN's sole responsibility was to deliver the stream to all the users who requested it, no matter their geographic location.

Live streaming lets you deliver critical information or time-sensitive events as a near real-time experience for Internet viewers. It is one of streaming media's strengths. You don't have to begin with large and complex events like Tiger Woods. Start small. As you investigate webcasting further, you will easily grasp the basic production concepts of getting your content live on the web.

Dan Rayburn is one of the most experienced individuals in the area of streaming media business models, strategy, industry foresight, hardware and software products, delivery methods, and cutting-edge technology solutions. You can contact Dan via his website at http://www.danrayburn.com.

5 Alternative Systems & Advanced Topics

Terms to Know

Standard: A standard is an agreed-upon set of principles and methods to achieve a technical task. The MPEG set of standards is an example.

MPEG: The Motion Picture Experts Group (MPEG) is a body of engineers and organizations that define the MPEG audio and video technical standards.

Open source: The open source philosophy and practice of software engineering permits anyone using a piece of software to view and modify the source code, thus revealing and possibly changing the software's methods. In the proprietary model, usually practiced by commercial enterprises, viewing and modifying the source code violates the software's license.

SMIL: Synchronized Multimedia Integration Language (SMIL) is an XML-compliant, open standard markup language designed to integrate still images, text, and advanced interactivity with streaming audio and video.

Peer-to-peer (or P2P): Peer-to-peer networking is a simple network architecture wherein all the computers on the network have equal status. Some streaming media solutions use peer-to-peer networking to manage bandwidth more efficiently.

Taking the Streaming Roads Less Traveled

We've all daydreamed about chucking it all, packing the family, and starting over. The daydreams occur when something about what we're doing at the moment doesn't feel quite right, though you can't put your finger on it. Maybe you've successfully implemented a streaming strategy at work, or put your home video online. But, you're thinking, there's got to be a better way or just a different way.

The wonderful thing about software is that there's always a different way of doing something. The universe of 1s and 0s is the most plastic ever conceived. In the streaming world, some people believe all codecs should work on any streaming platform. They shouldn't be limited to a single platform built by a private company. Others believe the source code behind the media players and streaming servers should be viewable by all. They distrust the inherent secrecy of proprietary software. Still others believe the dominant client/server architecture of streaming is wasteful. They prefer a model called peer-to-peer. All of these streaming practitioners have come up with solutions based on their own engineering principles and philosophical beliefs.

But your sense that something is out of kilter may be more prosaic. Audio and video is great, but can't we make this stuff more interesting, more interactive? Yes, you can. We'll talk about a couple of methods that go beyond sending a video signal to your grandma's laptop. Or you may remember the heyday of the 1990s' Internet bubble, when almost no one seemed to care about business models to back up the fancy new technologies, streaming included. Make a profit? Who cares! Well, believe it or not, solid business models are emerging in the streaming space, although it's still too early to tell whether any of them have long-term viability. Finally, when your boss asks you for some numbers to measure how your new investment in streaming is paying off, we'll have a method ready for you.

Although this book focuses on the streaming media methodologies that currently dominate the Internet, you don't have to limit yourself to them. That's the point of this chapter. You can dare to be different.

Home users and hobbyists: You can skip this chapter and not be the worse for wear. Unless you love to tinker with computers, including trying operating systems such as Linux, you may find this material hopelessly confusing. That's not to say you couldn't figure this stuff out. It just won't help you get the audio from your garage band recording on the Internet by the launch party tomorrow night. Read on, though, and you might be intrigued by your options.

Before You Veer Off the Main Highway

The writer William Least Heat Moon unfolded a road map one day and noticed something about lonely county roads and backwoods routes. He saw that many were colored blue, unlike the major trunk roads. He called a book about his treks on these "roads less traveled" *Blue Highways.* Sometimes he had grand adventures. Other times, he found himself alone and lonely.

If you decide to try alternative streaming solutions, go with your eyes open. Some of the advantages will appeal to you. But there are also important disadvantages. On the up side, you'll find yourself almost completely independent of proprietary systems, especially if you choose a fully open-source solution. (We'll talk about open source in detail below.) Some people chafe at the idea of dependency on a large corporation for a critical business system or personal service. They'd rather work within a community of equals dominated by an ethic of helpfulness and engineering elegance, rather than profit. Alternative streaming systems are worthy choices for individuals or small, flexible organizations willing to experiment and take risks in an unstructured environment.

On the other hand, if you prefer structure, or you work in an organization that has strong demands for accountability, a non-standard (read: non-proprietary) solution may create too much stress. Some people don't like working with tools that don't have the imprimatur of a Microsoft or Apple Computer. Others want a phone number to call or a printed manual from a bookstore, neither of which may be available for an alternative. You can mitigate potential conflict over non-standard solutions by educating your colleagues and bosses and demonstrating the organizational and financial value of an alternative streaming solution. In some cases, particularly in the technical arena, you can take advantage of the comfort of brand by using alternative solutions that people have heard about, though they may not have tried them.

MPEG: The Most Talked About Alternative to Proprietary Architectures

Every discussion about the relative merits of one streaming media solution over another includes an argument over MPEG-4 (pronounced "EM-peg four"), one of the handful of open standards for recording, storing, and sending digitized audio and video. MPEG-4 is the standard that directly affects streaming media. The argument revolves around whether MPEG-4 is an important factor in the development of streaming as a technology and an industry. But no one argues about the importance of MPEG as a group of standards.

What is a Standard?

A standard is a set of rules practitioners of a particular discipline agree to follow. In computer engineering, they often define the architecture of a particular type of solution. It's a little like agreeing on the general rules for constructing a building, but letting each architect design his or her application of the rules, as long as everyone can use the building. Non-streaming examples of computer standards include HTML, which is actually a set of rules for telling web browsers how to display information in a text file, among other things.

Open Standards vs. Proprietary Models

Open standards appeal to many computer engineers in part because of the transparent process behind the standard. A group of leading lights in a field get together in a public forum and hash out the rules that will govern anyone who wants to build something that works in that arena. Participation is voluntary. But a non-standard solution, even if it works, is often excluded by default if enough people adopt the standard.

Almost every popular piece of computer hardware is based in large part on some kind of engineering standard. The open standards allow different manufacturers to design different ways to solve a problem. If the solutions follow the standard, related pieces of hardware doing different jobs will work together. Success is not dependent on someone following a single manufacturer's way of doing things. Rather, success depends on sticking to a set of rules. Vendors compete on how they implement a standard, their pricing, and their support.

On the other hand, the history of technology in business is replete with stories of companies whose proprietary solutions became a standard without the blessing of a committee. The company and its owners/shareholders grew very rich when the marketplace made the rules, i.e., adopted the standard, which everyone else had to follow. This is a powerful incentive to create useful tools that solve real problems.

Microsoft is the best example in the software industry. Bill Gates made Windows the de facto standard for desktop and laptop computer operating systems. He used aggressive marketing, enjoyed technological prowess, and made the most of the opportunity presented by the dawn of the personal computer in the early 1980s.

The prospect of market dominance encourages all software companies to compete with each other for the best solution to a particular problem. In the ideal scenario, all potential customers eventually come to your "one-stop shop," and you reap the rewards of their long-term dependence on you. However, you cannot rest on your laurels. IBM is much less powerful than it was a generation ago because it missed the sweeping changes in computer technology that led to the dominance of the personal computer.

In the streaming world, the proprietary solution dominates. The leading companies, RealNetworks, Microsoft, and Apple Computer, ultimately want to "own" the streaming marketplace. Their software works pretty well and it's getting better all the time. They may not admit it, but they don't want to be tied to committee-created standards that can be slow to change in a dynamic environment, such as the Internet.

However, one can argue that the intense competition has held up the wider adoption of streaming. If these companies had followed open standards, some would say, people at home and at work who just want to hear some music or watch a sports highlight could simply click a button and listen or watch. They wouldn't have to worry about whether they have a particular media player or the latest codec or spend hours downloading stuff and other silliness. Shouldn't streaming be like turning on the radio or starting a car? Why not?

How Does MPEG-4 Fit?

The story of MPEG standards pre-dates streaming media. MPEG-1, adopted in 1992 by the Motion Pictures Experts Group (MPEG), defined how video is stored digitally on CD-ROM. At the time, CD-ROM was the multimedia rage. Before the Internet as we know it appeared, software companies believed the world would get its media fix via a plastic-coated metal platter, which had already taken over the music industry. MPEG-1 included MPEG Audio Layer III, an audio compression standard that would lead directly to the "MP3" file-sharing phenomenon of the late 1990s.

More MPEG standards followed. MPEG, which works under the direction of the International Standards Organization (ISO) and the International Electro-technical Committee (IEC), developed a new compression standard in 1994 dubbed MPEG-2. Now you could store video on a CD and play it back with "VCR-like" quality. MPEG-2 would become the basis of DVD and satellite TV technologies.

MPEG-4 arrived in 1998. It was originally designed for teleconferencing applications. But engineers started applying it to streaming media as an alternative to the rapid rise of proprietary technologies introduced by RealNetworks, Microsoft, and others a few years before. MPEG also grew into a way of packaging all kinds of data, such as text and still images. Interactivity is also a part of the standard. MPEG-4 is also discussed in the context of video distributed over wireless networks to Personal Digital Assistants (PDAs) and advanced cell phones. MPEG is more likely to have an impact in these delivery arenas in part because they're so new. In these areas, MPEG-4 doesn't have to play catch-up with the proprietary big boys.

MPEG is also branching out into standards that aren't directly related to delivering audio and video data. MPEG-7, for example, defines video and audio metadata. It was adopted in 2001. The goal is to make identification of audio and video material easier for search engines. See Table 5.1 for a list of the current MPEG standards either adopted or under discussion ("in dev").

Table 5.1. The MPEG standards

Standard	Adopted	Purpose
MPEG-1	1992	Store video on CD-ROM and early set-top boxes
MPEG Audio Layer III (MP3)	1992	Audio compression standard
MPEG-2	1994	Store VHS-quality video on CD. Used by DVD and satellite TV.
MPEG-3	1995	An early HDTV standard, later folded into MPEG-2
MPEG-4	1998	Video compression for teleconferencing, adapted for streaming media.
MPEG-7	2001	Defines metadata standards for sound and images
MPEG-21	(in dev)	An overarching standard covering all previous MPEG standards

The MPEG standards are an evolving group of engineering rules that govern digital storage of audio and video. The standard most important to streaming media is MPEG-4.

> **MPEG and Fees**
>
> Some private companies own patents related to the MPEG standards. Normally, people who want to develop products based on those patents pay a license fee to the patent owner. MPEG requires the fees to be fair, reasonable, and non-discriminatory. The fees compensate the companies that participate in the MPEG process.

Why MPEG Standards Are Important

Implementing a standard such as MPEG breaks the potential of a single company to dominate a marketplace. If every streaming media vendor supported MPEG-4 from the beginning to the end of the streaming process, for example, none could control the streaming market. You could encode a file into an MPEG-4 format with one vendor's tool and play it back with another. Users and producers are no longer locked into a particular way of doing things. Vendors would have to compete on other aspects of streaming, such as the availability of the latest Britney Spears video or major league baseball games.

More on MP3

As we mentioned above, the MPEG Audio Layer III standard is part of the original MPEG-1 standard for storing video on CD-ROM. Don't confuse MP3 with MPEG-3, which is a defunct High Definition Television (HDTV) standard that was folded into MPEG-2. Software manufacturers have developed tools to encode audio files into MP3 format, which has become a popular streaming media format as well as file storage format.

MP3 first gained notoriety when college students started sharing music files encoded into the format. The files were far smaller than the original files on their CDs and maintained most of the musical quality. Most CDs can store a little more than an hour's worth of music. With MP3, you can store up to 12 hours of high-fidelity audio. You could put hundreds, perhaps thousands of songs on a CD. The compression also led to the popularity of MP3 for portable digital music players and to MP3 streaming solutions, especially on peer-to-peer networks. Streaming MP3s also support standard encoding features such as multiple bit rates ranging from 8 kilobytes per second to 1.5 megabytes per second.

More on MPEG-4

MPEG-4 is usually discussed in the context of audio and video delivery. But it actually covers all types of media that could be delivery over a computer network.

MPEG-4 is a set of tools. The MPEG-4 video tool is only one of many in the toolbox.

MPEG-4 supports encoding at very low bit rates, starting at 2 kilobytes per second for audio and 5 kilobytes per second for video. High bit rates are also supported: 64 Kbps for CD-quality audio and up to 5 megabytes per second for video. MPEG-4 is "transport-agnostic," meaning you can use practically any protocol to deliver MPEG-4 files. MPEG-4 supports intellectual property protection to combat piracy. It's also backward compatible with other major existing standards. An upcoming version of the MPEG-4 standard will include a new file format, tentatively called "mp4."

How the Major Streaming Media Vendors Support MPEG Standards

The Big 3+1 streaming media vendors (RealNetworks, Microsoft, Apple Computer, and newcomer Macromedia) support MPEG standards to one degree or another. Here's how their support shakes out.

RealNetworks: The pioneer streaming media company is committed to a proprietary software model where it can gain competitive advantage through technological advances. But it also supports serving, creation, and playback of MPEG files. The company hopes to dominate the market by supporting virtually every streaming media format, including competitors' formats.

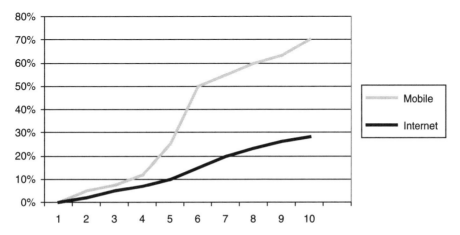

Figure 5.1 This chart describes MPEG's market penetration from the standard's introduction in 1992 through 2002. The top line is mobile streaming. The lower line is streaming media on broadband connections. (Data source: The MPEG Industry Forum)

RealNetworks Encoders and MPEG

Producers should note that RealNetworks' free encoder does not support MPEG encoding. You'll need to purchase the Xing MPEG Encoder if you're interested in MPEG encoding with RealNetworks products.

Microsoft: The ultimate proprietary software company is by its nature lukewarm to standards it cannot control. This leads to an inconsistent and contradictory implementation of these standards. The company supports MP3 file playback. But it has its own implementation of the MPEG-4 format, developed before the standard was finalized. Microsoft uses the term "MPEG-4" to describe this codec, but files created with the codec do not always play in competitors' media players. (One of the purposes of MPEG is cross-platform compatibility.) However, third-party software vendors have built plug-ins to Windows Media Player that allow playback of their MPEG implementations. In late 2003, Microsoft submitted its Windows Media 9 video compression technology to the Society of Motion Picture and Television Engineers (SMPTE) for adoption as a compression standard.

Apple Computer: Apple is the most aggressive among the Big 3+1 in touting its support of MPEG standards, especially MPEG-4. The company notes that the MPEG group chose the QuickTime file format as the "foundation" for the MPEG-4 standard. The company sees MPEG support as a key differentiator for its products, distinguishing it from its rivals, RealNetworks and Microsoft.

Macromedia: The Flash MX creator is the new kid on the streaming block, and its MPEG strategy is fuzzy. It supports MP3, but not MPEG-4. It may not need to support the video format at the moment, given the extreme ubiquity of its Flash Player. However, Macromedia may change its mind if its main customers, designers and web developers, demand MPEG-4 support.

Open Source: An Alternative to Proprietary Systems

Most consumers and businesses use software created by companies eager to keep their methodologies secret or tightly protected by intellectual property law. These laws are an important part of capitalism. If companies could not benefit exclusively from their ideas, they'd have little incentive to come up with these ideas. And keeping their methods secret helps companies maintain an edge in the marketplace.

However, some people view the software world as another kind of marketplace, where ideas are debated publicly. The best ideas survive, while the rest are discarded. And they say no one should own the mechanisms behind products that have become a central, almost indispensable part of our lives.

Imagine a different history of the internal combustion engine. What if the inventors never shared the ideas and methods behind their creation? What if Henry Ford kept his ideas secret, yet managed to sell hundreds of millions of vehicles? And what if his competitors held only small parts of the car market? The consumer would be completely tied to his company for maintenance and new models. You couldn't tinker with the motor in your backyard to make it run better to suit your own particular needs or taste. And the cost of switching to a different manufacturer could outweigh the benefits.

Proponents of the "open source" model of software believe that placing ideas before a community leads to better software for everyone. They believe everyone should have a chance to view and modify the "source code," the ideas and methods executed by software developers in programming languages such as C++ or Visual Basic. Tens of thousands of developers around the world create websites, post on newsgroups, and write to Internet e-mail lists about their ideas. They criticize other ideas and propose new solutions. Often, ad hoc teams grow out of a common interest in solving a problem, and in some cases, these teams, even individuals, have changed the software world.

The "Free" in "Freeware"

Some people prefer to use the term "freeware," rather than "open source." Freeware means that the source code is "free" for anyone to view, and "free" from the normal constraints of intellectual property law, including some provisions of copyright law. The "free" in freeware does not refer to the software's cost, although it's true that freeware/open source software can be downloaded and used at no charge.

Open Source Success Stories

The most famous example of the open source model is Linux. Finnish computer science student Linus Torvalds created Linux in the early 1990s because he wanted a Unix operating system for his IBM personal computer. Building on the ideas of others, he wrote an operating system, got it working, and shared the source code with some like-minded programmers on a computer bulletin board. He incorporated the suggestions of other programmers and posted the results. The project began to snowball.

The world of computer science is peppered with egomaniacs and bullies. Torvalds did not fit the mold. He brought a unique humbleness and ability to facilitate conversations missing from many discussions about software. He was also a good engineer. Furthermore, his operating system had strong networking features, which made it ideal for the new world of the Internet. First academic institutions, then new Internet businesses started by former students, started using Linux for their Internet servers. The operating system continued to improve, and it now accounts for a large chunk of servers directly connected to the Internet. Today, Torvalds still directs the development of the Linux kernel, the core part of Linux, which now includes thousands of utilities and applications, all available as open source software.

One of those applications accounts for two-thirds of the web servers on the Internet. You'll remember that a web server is the software that delivers a web page to you when you request it with your web browser. In 1995, the most popular web server was public domain software designed by Rob McCool at the National Center for Supercomputing Applications at the University of Illinois. But many webmasters had developed their own extensions and bug fixes to what was cryptically called the "HTTP daemon." A group got together and organized all the bug fixes, sometimes called "patches." The result was a web server called "Apache," as in "a patchy server." Apache is the single most successful open source application on the Internet.

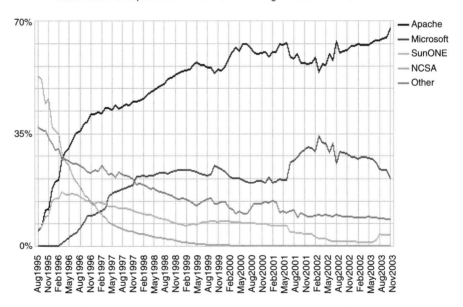

Market Share for Top Servers Across All Domains August 1995 - November 2003

Figure 5.2 The Apache web server (top line) accounts for nearly 70 percent of all web servers deployed on the Internet. (Source: Netcraft. The latest figures are available at http://www.netcraft.com)

Advantages and Disadvantages of Open Source Tools

The open source model of development has some distinct advantages and disadvantages. Some of the most important advantages include the following:

- An opportunity to know exactly how a mission-critical piece of software works
- Ability to modify the software to suit your particular needs
- Up-front costs often close to zero
- Licensing often extremely liberal (See box below on licensing.)
- Support available in two basic forms:
  - Vendors specializing in open source software support
  - Participation in the open source community.

The disadvantages of open source software include

- Usually requires strong knowledge of operating systems, especially Unix and its clones, including Linux
- Rarely backed by a major organization with large resources. The exceptions are the major names, such as Linux or Apache.
- Community support can be spotty and response times irregular or infrequent
- Good documentation can be difficult to find. Again, exceptions to this are the popular open source solutions, such as Linux.

Open Source Licensing

The document that makes open source "open" is the license. As we said in Chapter 4, you don't actually own the software installed on your computer. Rather, you own a license to use it and the license sets the rules for its use. There are several types of open source licenses. The most popular is called the General Public License (GPL). All open source licenses grant you the right to view the source code of your software and make changes as you see fit. Differences often occur in permissions you have to distribute changes. If you want to learn more about open source licensing, visit the website for the non-profit Open Source Initiative, http://www.opensource.org/

Open Source Streaming Solutions

Most of the open source work in the streaming realm has focused on the server side. The best example is Darwin, a variant of the QuickTime Streaming Server. The project is sponsored by Apple Computer. Darwin has many of the features of the QuickTime Streaming Server, and it runs on Mac OS X, Linux, and Microsoft Windows NT/Server 2000. Darwin serves MP3 audio and MPEG-4 video files to QuickTime Player. RealPlayer and Windows Media Player can play MPEG files served with Darwin if users install the EnvivioTV MPEG plug-in.

RealNetworks has also taken up the open source banner. The company has created a community of software developers around its "Helix DNA Platform," which is a facet of its effort to create a universal digital media platform that includes streaming. RealNetworks allows participating developers to view the source code of Helix clients, encoders, and servers, and modify it for their own use. Developers can also suggest changes to Helix code for the wider Helix community. RealNetworks has written special open source licenses that allow the company to retain property rights while taking advantages of the "marketplace of ideas" concept at the heart of open source development.

Peer-to-Peer (P2P) Streaming

The most common network architecture for streaming media is client/server. Numerous software clients on computer desktops contact a central server, which delivers the data to the client. It looks a lot like the familiar "one transmitter to many receivers" model in over-the-air broadcasting.

But streaming producers have a second network architecture choice: peer-to-peer or "P2P." All the computers, or "workstations," in a peer-to-peer network have more or less equal status and share resources, such as files and printers. There's no hierarchy implied with a centralized server. The difference can be subtle. If you have a computer hooked up to a printer, and all the other workstations use the same printer, the first computer can be called a "server." If the "server" also performs workstation tasks, such as word processing, then it's technically not a server, because it's not dedicated to server-related tasks. Many small businesses and most home networks use a peer-to-peer model.

The difference becomes clearer when we talk about peer-to-peer streaming. Most notably, peer-to-peer architecture has the ability to overcome the most important streaming resource problem, bandwidth. In the client/server model, dozens, hundreds, or thousands of clients may contact a single server all at once. If dozens, hundreds, or thousands of clients contact your server all at once, your bandwidth could be overwhelmed and your whole system could fail.

In the peer-to-peer model, there's no division of labor; computers consume and serve/relay streams at the same time. Bandwidth needs are distributed equally among all the client machines, and adding new clients doesn't necessarily lead to capacity problems. In other words, the bandwidth bottleneck is removed. Peer-to-peer, or "distributed content," advocates say many computers over many small connections can do the same work as a single computer with one fat connection at lower costs and higher return for the content provider.

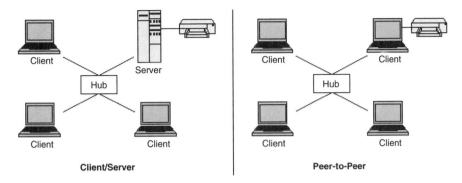

Figure 5.3   The two main network architectures, client/server and peer-to-peer.

The main problem with peer-to-peer is not technical, but political. Much of the illegal sharing of music files since the dawn of the Internet has happened over peer-to-peer networks, which are much harder to control than client/server networks. In the client/server model, all the content files are stored in one place, the server. In the peer-to-peer model, the content files can be shared on any, perhaps all, of the participating computers. Music companies and other purveyors of copyrighted material (including software companies) lose tight control over their intellectual property on peer-to-peer networks. Most intellectual property business models depend on ownership and control of the product by a single individual or corporate entity.

Another problem has to do with "free riders." The success of peer-to-peer architecture, including streaming, depends on users who are willing to relay streams. However, a large portion of peer-to-peer users consume files and streams without passing them to the next user. These "free riders" take advantage of the benefits of peer-to-peer streaming without contributing to the community effort.

Two Popular Peer-to-Peer Streaming Implementations

Several software companies have developed peer-to-peer streaming solutions. Here are two of the most popular, SHOUTcast and ICEcast.

SHOUTcast—Prospective online broadcasters interested in SHOUTcast start by installing an MP3 media player such as Winamp for Windows or Audion for the Mac. To broadcast a stream, you install a SHOUTcast Distributed Network Audio Server, which allows you to receive and relay streams to other peers. As with any streaming, it's important that you have a robust connection to the Internet, such as cable/DSL. To find out more, visit http://www.shoutcast.com.

ICEcast—ICEcast is one of the leading open source peer-to-peer streaming solutions. It's completely community based, and it supports an open source streaming format called "Ogg Vorbis" that can be played by the Winamp player. The ICEcast architecture is similar to SHOUTcast, but ICEcast runs only on Linux. To learn more, visit http://www.icecast.org.

Synchronized Multimedia Integration Language

The realm of streaming media tends to be limited to sending audio and video over the Internet in real time. However, you can stream other kinds of data, such as static images and text, side-by-side with audio and video. This allows you to create different kinds of time-based media experiences that take advantage of the efficiency of streaming technology. The most flexible tool for managing a variety of streaming data types in the same application is Synchronized Multimedia Integration Language, or SMIL.

We like to think of SMIL (pronounced "smile") as a markup language for multimedia. It looks a lot like HTML with the addition of tags that let you time events. With the timing tags, you decide when certain things happen, such as the start and end times of an audio clip within a larger timeline. Producers can also incorporate links within a SMIL presentation for interactivity, similar to links in a web page. SMIL is XML-compliant, meaning it follows XML's rules for tag construction. SMIL applications play in RealPlayer and QuickTime Player. Windows Media Player does not support SMIL.

A Simple SMIL Example

One of the most common SMIL implementations is the slideshow. It's also the easiest to understand. Let's say you want to create a narrated streaming slideshow of your family camping trip to the Grand Canyon. You've created JPEG graphics files out of your photos with a graphics programs such as Adobe Photoshop. You've arranged the photos in the correct order and recorded a simple narration. Open a text editor, such as Notepad, and type the following code:

```
<smil>
    <head>
    <layout>
        <root-layout id="root" width="320"
            height="240" background-color="black"/>
        <region id="slides" width="320"
            height="240"/>
    </layout>
    </head>
```

```
<body>
<par>
<seq>
      <img src="photo1.jpg" region="slides"
         dur="5s"/>
      <img src="photo2.jpg" region="slides"
         dur="15s"/>
      <img src="photo3.jpg" region="slides"
         dur="10s" />
</seq>
<audio src="narration.rm" />
</par>
</body>
</smil>
```

Let's go through each of the tags.

`<smil></smil>`—These are the opening and closing container tags to all SMIL files, similar to the `<html></html>` tags in a web page.

`<head></head>`—These define the header for the file, which is primarily for setting basic layout parameters.

`<layout></layout>`—The `layout` tag holds information about the layout.

`<root-layout/>`—The `root-layout` parameter tag lays the foundation for the rest of the presentation. In this case, it tells the media player that the presentation is 320 pixels wide and 240 pixels tall. It also sets the main background color to black. Note the lack of a closing container for this tag.

`<region/>`—The `region` tag, in this case, tells the media player where the slides should play within the `root-layout`. For our camping trip slideshow, the slides take up the whole `root-layout` area. We could make the region smaller, but not larger. Don't forget to give the `region` a name, signaled by the `id` parameter.

`<body></body>`—The `body` tags, similar to the `body` tags in HTML, hold the data types to be displayed.

`<par></par>`—The `par` tags tell the media player about a group of items that play in "parallel," or simultaneously. In this case, we have only one group of items, so we need only one set of `par` tags.

`<seq></seq>`—The `seq` tags define the items that play in "sequence," that is, one after the other.

`<img/>`—The three `img` tags in this example tell the media player which of our camping trip photos to play and in what order. The `src` parameter identifies the image. The `region` parameter places the photo in a region defined in the `<layout></layout>` container, in this case, "slides," which is our only region. The `dur` tag (short for "duration") tells the player how long to show each photo. The first photo is displayed for 5 seconds, the second for 15 seconds, and the third for 10 seconds.

`<audio/>`—We put the audio narration after the closing `seq` tag, and before the closing `par` tag. This tells the media player to play the audio file while the photos cycle through their order. We've used a file encoded in RealNetworks format for this example. But you could use a QuickTime streaming audio file as well.

Playing the SMIL Slideshow

Save the SMIL file with the extension `.smi`, as in `slideshow.smi`. (Some people like to use the extension `.smil`. Both `.smi` and `.smil` will work.) Upload the SMIL file to your RealNetworks Helix or QuickTime Streaming server, and place it in the same directory as your JPEG photos and audio narration file. Then load the URL to the SMIL file in your RealPlayer or QuickTime Player. The URL will look something like this:

`rtsp://streaming.server.com/myslideshow/slideshow.smi`

You can also put this URL into a metafile and put the metafile on your web server. It will work just like a metafile to an audio or video file.

Slideshows: A Powerful, Underused Tool

We think slideshows are one of the most powerful and underused multimedia applications on the Internet. Let's say you have a video, but you're worried about the bandwidth capabilities of your audience. Consider taking some screenshots from the video and creating a SMIL slideshow, using the audio track from the video as the timeline. A number of JPEG graphics files paired with a low bit rate audio file take up much less bandwidth than a full-fledged video file. Now you can offer a slideshow that performs well on low-bandwidth connections, as well as a standard video for folks with more bandwidth. And you've found two uses for the same content.

RealNetworks and Apple QuickTime Extensions

The SMIL language is governed by a standard similar to other standards, such as MPEG. However, RealNetworks and Apple Computer have added non-standard "extensions" to SMIL. RealNetworks, in particular, has created a whole range of extra functionality for SMIL presentations, such as RealPix and RealText.

Figure 5.4 A simple SMIL slideshow. Note the names in the lower half of the presentation. Clicking these takes the user to specific points in the slideshow timeline.

- *RealPix*—The RealPix functionality in RealPlayer allows producers to add video-like effects to static images, such as wipes, fades, and cross-fades.
- *RealText*—The RealText functionality lets you add features including text crawls and closed captioning to presentations.

Note that RealNetworks' SMIL extensions work only in RealPlayer, not in other media players.

QuickTime's SMIL extensions are not as elaborate as RealNetworks', although they allow some fine-tuning of QuickTime Player behavior. Both sets of extensions require some advanced knowledge of XML syntax.

Learning How to SMIL

The SMIL section in this chapter is meant as a brief introduction to the language. If you're interested in learning how to write SMIL applications, we suggest visiting the RealNetworks or QuickTime web sites and studying the documentation in detail. There are also a few third-party software packages that can get you started. But in the case of SMIL, there's no substitute for getting your hands dirty with the code.

SMIL's Main Drawback

As we said above, the only media players that support SMIL are RealPlayer and QuickTime Player. Of course, that leaves out one of the heavyweights, Windows Media Player. If you're interested in producing a SMIL application, go back to your audience analysis in Chapter 3. Will a large share of your audience be using Windows Media Player? If so, you may need to rethink your SMIL plans.

The PowerPoint Alternative

Microsoft PowerPoint has become the default standard for creating dynamic computer presentations containing images, text, audio, and video. Later versions of PowerPoint allow you to broadcast a live or on-demand streaming version of a PowerPoint presentation to as many as 50 desktop computers from your desktop, assuming your audience has Windows Media Player. PowerPoint streaming works fine for small-scale intranet broadcasts where high audio and video quality are not an issue.

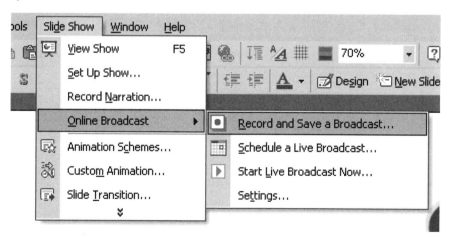

Figure 5.5   You can create a streaming version of a PowerPoint presentation and broadcast it directly from your desktop or laptop computer.

To stream PowerPoint presentations, you record an audio narration while you flip through your slides as if you were delivering the presentation before an audience. You can use an inexpensive computer microphone for your narration or even a web cam if you prefer video. Here's the basic procedure for creating an on-demand presentation in PowerPoint 2000:

1. Create your slides with PowerPoint.
2. Click SlideShow->Online Broadcast->Set Up and Schedule and click OK.
3. In the Schedule a New Broadcast window, click the Description tab.
4. Enter a title, description, name of the speaker, and a contact email address or telephone number.
5. Click the Broadcast Settings tab.
6. Check Audio or Video.
7. Check the Recording checkbox and type a file name for the file, which will be in Windows Media format.
8. Click the Server Options button.
9. Choose a shared location, which is a shared directory on your own machine or a web server where PowerPoint will save the web pages for your presentation.
10. Click OK.
11. Click OK again on the Schedule a New Broadcast window.
12. Click SlideShow->Online Broadcast->Begin Broadcast. The program will walk you through an audio or video check, depending on your setup.
13. To play back the on-demand presentation, load the URL to the presentation in your browser window.
14. Tell your audience the location of your file. (If your organization uses Microsoft Exchange email server, this may be done automatically.)

All the usual constraints of streaming apply, such as bandwidth. For more details, consult your PowerPoint documentation.

Streaming Business Opportunities and Models

The end of the 1990s' Internet bubble left a single question still unanswered: Can anyone make money with these new networking technologies? No one in the streaming arena has come up with a slam-dunk formula for a sustainable business model. But that doesn't mean the potential for profit went away with the last bull market of the 20th century. In fact, marketers have identified an entirely new market segment called "streamies," which is growing as fast as cable and DSL connectivity providers can hook them up. According to a 2003 report by Arbitron/Edison Media Research, a marketing research firm, 50 million

Americans tried streaming media in a given month. Businesses large and small are now positioning themselves to benefit from the demands of streamies.

The Streaming Media Consumer

Arbitron publishes a study twice a year that tries to nail down the "streamie," the individual who listens to or watches some form of streaming media. The second study the company published in 2003 came up with these characteristics:

- More likely male than female
- Mostly age 25–45
- Has a full-time job
- Has a household income of around $50,000
- Largely Caucasian
- Better than 50-50 chance of having broadband at home
- Spent $861 online in the past 12 months

The average weekly streamie spends almost 2-1/2 hours a day online. In contrast, only 7 percent of streamies thumbed through a newspaper last week.

Programming Preferred by Streamies

A study by the Cable and Telecommunications Association for Marketing (CTAM) found that streamies are interested in particular forms of programming. More than a third of streamies are touring travel destinations or listening to Internet radio. Twenty-six percent watch online news clips. See Figure 5.6 for more of their results.

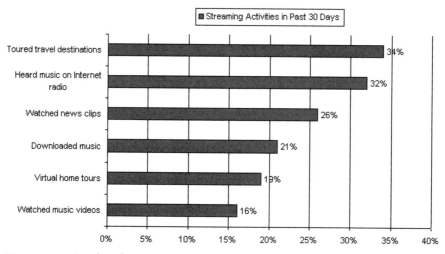

Figure 5.6 Results of a 2002 streaming media programming study by the Cable and Telecommunications Association for Marketing. (Source: CTAM)

Four Potential Business Models

You now have a picture of the average streaming media consumer and his or her viewing habits. What are some ways of serving that market and making a profit? We'd like to offer four basic business models to spark your thinking.

Content creation—Streamies won't go online if there's nothing to watch or hear. They're looking for compelling programming. Most streaming media content these days is re-purposed from over-the-air or cable broadcasts. In the case of music, they are re-purposed music tracks that would have been heard exclusively on CDs or radio stations a few years ago.

However, Arbitron advises streaming media producers to develop new programs to spur growth and create "buzz" that will encourage more visitors to play streams. We're reminded of cable television in the late 1970s and early 1980s, when all-movie channels such as Showtime and HBO attracted more viewers to cable TV. In 1980, cable TV entrepreneur Ted Turner created CNN, the world's first 24-hour television news channel, something completely new in television news broadcasting. CNN sparked a consumer rush to cable TV and turned it into the media force we know today. We can't say whether a new streaming program will build a new "CNN effect." But no such program has appeared on the horizon so far.

Content delivery—If someone did create a wildly popular streaming media program, someone would have to host and deliver those streams. As of today, most web hosting companies offer some streaming media hosting as part of a larger package. The streaming services add incremental revenue. But a few businesses make streaming media delivery a core service. Real Broadcast Network (RBN), for example, is a division of RealNetworks. RBN's sole purpose is streaming media delivery. Other businesses also focus exclusively on streaming media delivery, whether it's simple hosting of files or soup-to-nuts production of a live streaming media event. They serve both Internet and intranet audiences as streaming contractors. As stream volume increases and technical demands grow, more streaming specialists are likely to emerge.

Advertising—Contrary to popular belief, the advertising model on the Internet is not dead. The question has become, What kind of online advertising works? The banner ad, the first widespread form of website advertising, is in decline. According to Arbitron, the proportion of online users who have clicked on a banner ad has fallen steadily since the summer of 2000. The days of other ad forms may also be numbered. Arbitron says 65 percent of Internet users find pop-up ads annoying. One quarter of web users have installed a program to block pop-ups.

In contrast, Arbitron says only 3 percent of people online object to commercials during an audio or video stream. Only 2 percent dislike streaming ads played before an on-demand stream. Why the difference? Perhaps the audience is accustomed to these kinds of interruptions, since they see/hear them all the

Potential Value of the Internet Audio Audience
If sold as a single radio network today

($ Million/Year)

CPM	Units per hour									
	1	2	3	4	5	6	7	8	9	10
$1.00	$4	$9	$13	$17	$22	$26	$30	$34	$39	$43
$1.50	$6	$13	$19	$26	$32	$39	$45	$52	$58	$65
$2.00	$9	$17	$26	$34	$43	$52	$60	$69	$77	$86
$2.50	$11	$22	$32	$43	$54	$65	$75	$86	$97	$108
$3.00	$13	$26	$39	$52	$65	$77	$90	$103	$116	$129
$3.50	$15	$30	$45	$60	$75	$90	$105	$120	$136	$151
$4.00	$17	$34	$52	$69	$86	$103	$120	$138	$155	$172
$4.50	$19	$39	$58	$77	$97	$116	$136	$155	$174	$194
$5.00	$22	$43	$65	$86	$108	$129	$151	$172	$194	$215

How to read: *CPM* indicates the cost of buying 1000 impressions. *Units per hour* means the number of commercial aired per hour. Select a CPM and the number of commercials per hour to determine the annual value of the Internet audio broadcast market. Example: With current Internet audio broadcast audience levels, a $5.00 CPM with five commercials per hour would yield a $108 million Internet audio broadcast and market.

Figure 5.7 Potential cost-per-thousand (CPM) value of the Internet audience is sold as a single audience. (Source: Arbitron/Edison Media Research, 2003)

time on cable and over-the-air broadcasts. Whatever the reason, these figures suggest that ads on streams won't alienate streamies the way other ad forms do. Arbitron recommends that streaming producers consider advertising as a viable revenue model, and that advertisers, especially those who want to reach techno-savvy, upscale audiences, take streaming seriously as a communications channel.

Ad Insertion Features

RealNetworks, Microsoft, and Apple Computer offer special features with their streaming services that allow producers to insert advertising seamlessly into streams. Each vendor has its own methodology, including tracking mechanisms for judging an ad's effectiveness. Check each vendor's website for detailed information.

Subscription—The subscription model for Internet content is one of the most controversial. It's no surprise that Internet audiences prefer free access to content. Arbitron says audiences also prefer ad-supported content over content they have to pay for directly. That signals an opportunity for advertisers, if they can find the right delivery model. But another study has found that pay-for-play may have a future. The Cable and Telecommunications Association for Marketing found the following in 2002:

- 27 percent of streamies were somewhat or very likely to pay for full-length movies.
- 23 percent were somewhat or very likely to pay for streamed music.
- 20 percent were somewhat or very likely to pay for live sports events.

Here's an important clue to understanding the potential: CTAM found that around a quarter to a third of people open to buying a streaming subscription buy premium cable services. They're used to paying extra for special content. Put another way, the general outline of the basic/premium cable channel model may work on the Internet.

The streaming heavyweights are taking this potential seriously. All three are offering some form of subscription service. RealNetworks has placed the biggest bet. In its third-quarter 2003 report to investors, the company counted 1.15 million subscribers to its suite of content services. Each subscriber pays $9.95 per month for exclusive access to music streams, video streams, games, and a media guide. Furthermore, streaming vendors are building partnerships with content owners. Major League Baseball offers access to baseball game audio via RealNetworks' "SuperPass" package. CinemaNow offers full-length movies through a premium service in Windows Media Player.

Exclusivity is the key. Again, cable provides the model. For a subscriber to sign on, he or she must see the programming as unique, compelling, and unavailable anywhere else. If the programming is available on another "channel" for free or at lower cost, the viewer will abandon the subscription.

Authentication Features

As with ad insertion, the major streaming vendors offer methods in their systems to authenticate subscribers to streaming services, usually with a username and password.

Streaming and Content Management Software

Many mid-sized and large enterprises that publish lots of content use a content management tool such as Vignette's "V" series and Interwoven's TeamSite product. If you plan to manage a large number of websites with lots of streams, and you think you need a content management system, ask a potential vendor how its product incorporates and manages streaming media.

Success Measurement

Every serious business model requires a method for measuring return on invest-ment. Media owners typically measure the success of properties, such as radio shows and TV sitcoms, with ratings. Streaming media also requires measure-ment of stream quality and the user experience. Online technology provides the most detailed types of data for gauging by storing information from each click in a log that can by analyzed in near real time.

Log Analysis

Every streaming media server has a logging feature. The logs are text files that store information about the stream, such as the IP address of the computer that viewed the stream, the codec for the stream, and the version of the media player. The text files can often be enormous, especially on a busy site. Here's a single entry from a Windows Media Server 4.1 stream log:

```
192.168.0.2 2001-03-05 00:29:09 carl.elltel.net
mms://134.121.239.122/stream.wma 0 4292073 1 200
{2801dd60-63ce-11d3-86b7-ce1b99aa2d9d} 6.4.7.1112
en-US — — MPLAYER2.EXE 6.4.7.1112 Windows_98 4.10.
0.1998 Pentium 0 494 4 http TCP Windows_Media_
Audio_V2 — — 0 0 0 0 0 0 0 0 0 0 0 0 100
134.121.239.122 videoserver2.urel.wsu.edu 15 0
```

Here's what some of the fields mean:

`192.168.0.2`—The IP address of the requesting media player.

`2001-03-05 00:29:09`—The date and time of the request.

`mms://192.168.0.1/stream.wma`—The URL of the requested stream.

`6.4.7.1112`—The version of the media player.

`Windows_Media_Audio_V2`—The version of the audio codec.

Streaming producers can parse these logs looking for patterns or trends in streaming media usage. For example, does the traffic vary or peak during certain times of the day? Is the use of older media players falling over time? Which streams are more popular than others? Some of the fields record data that net-work administrators can use to diagnose problems or optimize the network for better streaming performance.

If you've done analysis of web server logs, you'll notice some similarities. Streaming server log formats are based on the standard web server log format. But there's no standard streaming log format. In fact, at least with RealNetworks' server logs, you can set the types of data you want to record on top of a basic set of data fields. Streaming logs store data web server logs do not, such as the amount of time a media player played a streaming file.

You have two choices if you want to analyze your streaming server logs. You can build your own tools, parsing logs with scripts written in the Perl language, for example. Your homegrown tool could store the data in a database for more flexible types of analysis, and you could build a web page interface to allow other folks to monitor traffic.

Your other choice is a third-party tool. EnScaler's Lariat is one of the oldest streaming log analysis applications on the market. WebTrends, one of the leading website analysis companies, offers streaming log analysis features in its enterprise services.

Audience Measurement

Log files provide detailed information about the stream. But logs can't tell you anything about the person *playing* the stream. You could infer preferences. For example, if you see the same IP address requesting the same set of football video highlights week after week, you could say the person likes to watch a lot of football. But this kind of inference is prone to all kinds of errors. How do you know it's the same person every week?

Streaming producers should pair log analysis with standards types of market analysis, such as telephone surveys and focus groups. Compare the results of your marketing studies against your log files. Do the types of files stored in your server logs match the preferences expressed by individuals in your surveys? Do focus groups say they watch movie trailers all the way through, but your logs show people stop the stream after a few seconds? An integrated approach using a variety of tools is likely to provide the most accurate answers.

Stream Quality Measurement

Streaming server logs can also give you some insight into the quality of the user experience and the ability of your network to deliver the streams in a reliable way. Networking gurus and programmers can design software tools that make use of the error reporting in the Real Time Protocol (RTP), assuming the client is using RTSP to request the stream. These tools are very complex to build and maintain.

Many streaming producers who want to monitor quality over the long term make use of content monitoring services, such as Keynote. These companies use automated tools that contact your streaming server on a regular basis from several locations and report reliability statistics. You can use these to find bottlenecks in your network, for example.

Calculating a Return on Investment

Your return on your streaming media investment depends on how you use it and its purpose. It's extremely important to see streaming media as one facet of a

Use Your Own Products

All this gobbledegook about log analysis and focus groups and auto-mated monitoring isn't going to make a whit of difference if you don't click your own streams once in a while. It's stunning how streaming producers forget to click links on their own web pages. Then when they do, and something is broken, they act surprised. First rule of quality assurance: *Use your own products!* At least pretend to be an average user to get a feel for what his or her streaming life is like.

complete communications strategy. It's a new tool, but it shouldn't be the only tool in the toolbox. At this stage of the game, streaming media provides incre-mental benefits to people trying to deliver a message to certain audiences. But streaming media won't save a strategy that's flawed from the start. It certainly won't save a broken business model.

Having said that, streaming media can provide a tangible return almost immediately. Let's take the example of employee training, one of the fastest growing applications of streaming. In a study conducted in 2001, *Streaming Media* magazine found several cases where streaming saved a significant amount of money in training costs:

- A network equipment maker reduced training costs by a factor of seven. The company spends $10 million on streaming to send an average of 8.5 hours of content annually to its 40,000 employees, much of that in travel costs.
- A semiconductor manufacturer went from spending $500,000 per year for on-site training of its 500 new employees and distributors to $100,000 for streamed training.
- A major oil company keeps up with its corporate compliance require-ments through streaming. The company reaches 31,000 employees at 8,300 gas stations with one stream. Previously, it had to ship some 350,000 videotapes around the country.

According to the report, the same principles that apply to training apply to cor-porate communications. The content in this area is for employees, business part-ners, and customers, and includes such events as "the boss talking to the troops," human resources policy announcements, and financial disclosures.

We're not accountants, so we can't tell you how to figure return on invest-ment (ROI) in detail. But check out Figure 5.8 for some ideas on figuring out whether you're getting something for your streaming media money.

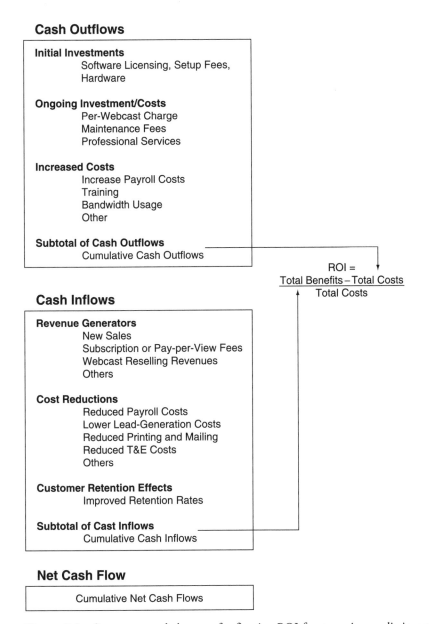

Figure 5.8 Some suggested elements for figuring ROI for streaming media investments. (Source: Yankee Group, 2002)

Chapter Summary

In this chapter, you learned about the major alternatives to the four main streaming media solutions. We discussed the MPEG standards, and how MP3 and MPEG-4 fit into the streaming landscape. We took you through the option of open source tools, such as the Darwin Streaming Server. We also showed you an alternative way of creating streaming experiences through SMIL and PowerPoint presentations. Another section discussed potential business models in the streaming arena. We hinted at some ways to gauge audience response to your streams through streaming server log analysis. Finally, we offered some thoughts on calculating a return on your streaming media investment.

Measuring Streaming Media Quality of Service

By Shai Berger

Performance measurement and monitoring have long been part of the game for websites. Many services measure basic uptime as well as the speed of complicated web-based transactions. These services address the needs of content owners who must make informed decisions about their infrastructure and hosting partners.

These same needs exist in streaming media. In fact, the increased complexity of streaming media—with its multiple formats, codecs, players, and its high bit rates—calls for even more rigorous testing. There are several solutions on the market for measuring and monitoring streaming media performance.

Encoding Quality vs. Delivery Quality

Let's first understand the difference between *encoding quality* and *delivery quality*. Both of these categories are important in giving your audience a high-quality experience. But they require different types of measurements and they are largely independent of each other. *Encoding quality* is concerned with how well your original audio and video is compressed and converted into a streaming format. The principal trade-off is the resulting bit rate vs. the resulting visual/audio quality. Once you have settled on an encoding strategy and converted your material to the appropriate format, the main concern shifts to *delivery quality*.

Measuring Delivery Quality

Objective data is key to ensuring reliable and high-quality delivery. You can get this data through your own internal processes or by working with a streaming measurement service. These services have a network of measurement computers (often called "agents") distributed around the world so that you get an accurate representation of how your audience is experiencing your content. Each agent performs regularly scheduled "checks" on your streams. They attempt to connect to the stream and play it, and they measure various aspects of the stream.

Working With a CDN

Many content owners outsource streaming delivery to a Content Delivery Network (CDN). Shop around and compare CDN quality metrics along with price and features. Most CDNs use internal tools to collect quality-of-service data. They will share this with you. However, an independent source of quality metrics is the only way to bring objective information to the table. Don't hesitate to ask for an SLA (Service Level Agreement) with your CDN. An SLA sets mutually agreed-upon benchmarks for performance. SLAs enforced by 3rd-party metrics are the most powerful tool a content owner has to ensure top-notch delivery by a CDN.

Basic Metrics

There are many ways to measure stream quality. The most basic metric is the Connection Success Rate (CSR), also called Availability. This is a percentage of the number of times a connection was established with the streaming server vs. total attempted checks. Another basic metric is Bit Rate. The average bit rate of data transfer achieved offers a comparison of actual bit rate received vs. encoded bit rate. This will let you know if your method of delivery has sufficient bandwidth for your content. It's also important to consolidate the information into a manageable and actionable form.

The Time Profile

A successful streaming experience for the audience is defined by the "time profile." Users will give up on content if forced to wait too long. A streaming transaction involves Connect Time (time between the initial

Continued

request for data by the media player and the start of buffering), Buffer Time (time used to build up the initial buffer of data for the stream), and Play Time (during which the agent will collect various metrics on the stream quality).

There may also be Rebuffer Time. Rebuffering pauses playback while the media player's buffer is refilled. It occurs when there is a decrease in the incoming bit rate of the stream. Rebuffering is an indication of an inconsistent connection. Rebuffer time should be zero in a properly configured system.

Our ultimate goal is to offer a high quality of service to a demanding audience. Objectively measuring the output of our streaming services on a sustained, regular basis helps us achieve that goal.

Shai Berger is the General Manager of Streaming Services at Keynote, where he leads the team responsible for Streaming Perspective, a leading streaming performance measurement product. Shai has a degree in Engineering Physics and a Master's degree in Applied Science from University of Toronto. For information about Keynote's streaming measurement services, write to shai.berger@keynote.com.

Resources

The following websites contain information and software related to streaming media.

Leading streaming media manufacturers:

- RealNetworks—http://www.realnetworks.com
- Microsoft— http://www.microsoft.com/windows/windowsmedia/
- Apple Computer—http://www.apple.com/quicktime/
- Macromedia—http://www.macromedia.com/

Media player download pages:

- RealNetworks—http://www.realnetworks.com/info/freeplayer/
- Microsoft—http://www.microsoft.com/windows/windowsmedia/9series/player.aspx
- Apple Computer—http://www.apple.com/quicktime/products/qt/(Use the "QuickTime Player" link.)
- Macromedia—http://www.macromedia.com/downloads/(Look for the "Macromedia Flash Player" link.)

Free encoder ("producer") download pages:

- RealNetworkshttp://www.realnetworks.com/products/producer/basic.html
- Microsoft—http://www.microsoft.com/windows/windowsmedia/9series/encoder/default.aspx
- Apple Computer—No free encoder here. Upgrade the player to a player/encoder.
- Macromedia—No free version. But a 30-day trial version is available. http://www.macromedia.com/software/flash/

Suggested free FTP clients:

- WS_FTP LE—http://www.ipswitch.com/downloads/index.html
- FTP Commander—http://www.internet-soft.com/ftpcomm.htm
- Cute FTP—http://www.cuteftp.com/cuteftp/

Open source software and information:

- Apache—http://www.apache.org. The home website for the most popular web server on the Internet.

- Darwin Streaming Server—http://developer.apple.com/darwin/projects/ streaming/. The Darwin Streaming Server project is supported by Apple Computer.
- ICEcast—http://www.icecast.org   Peer-to-peer streaming system.
- Linux—http://www.linux.org   One of many sites with information about this open source operating system.
- Open Source Initiative—http://www.opensource.org   The not-for-profit organization supporting open source software development.
- SHOUTcast—http://www.shoutcast.com   Peer-to-peer streaming system.

MPEG resources:

- MPEG.org—http://www.mpeg.org   Dozens of links and information about the MPEG standards.
- MP3—http://www.mpeg.org/MPEG/mp3.html   For MP3 information, visit MPEG.org's MP3 page.
- MPEG-4 Industry Forum (M4IF)—http://www.m4if.org   The main website for MPEG-4 supporters.

Places to buy audio and video recording equipment:

- Broadcast Supply Worldwide (audio)—http://www.bswusa.com/
- The Broadcast Store (video)—http://www.bcs.tv/
- Online auction sites, such as Ebay.com or Yahoo! Auctions at Yahoo.com.
- A local electronics store, such as Radio Shack or BestBuy, for small items you need immediately.

Publications:

- Digital Media Magazine (formerly Streaming Magazine)— http://www.digitalmediamagazine.net/
- Streaming Media—http://www.streamingmedia.com/
- Streaming Media Bible—http://www.streamingmediabible.com   The site for the definitive reference book on streaming media.

Other websites:

- American Federation of Television and Radio Artists (AFTRA)— http://www.aftra.com/Review rules for using actors and other artists in audio and video productions at this website for their union.
- Arbitron/Edison Media Research—http://www.arbitron.com   A rich source of information on streaming and digital media trends.

- NASA—http://www.nasa.gov   This is a good place to download public-domain AVI files to practice encoding.

- Synchronized Multimedia Integration Language (SMIL)—http://www.w3.org/AudioVideo   Check out this page at the W3C standards body for many resources on SMIL.

- Sorenson Media—http://www.sorenson.com   Learn more about the Sorenson codecs used in Flash MX.

Glossary

3-point lighting: The standard method of lighting a video subject, using a key light, a fill light, and a back light.

Analog: Describes data flowing in a continuous, often variable manner.

Artifacts: Lines, distortion, snow, or other unwanted data in a video image usually introduced by poor-quality equipment. Artifacts can appear in audio as odd sounds, dropouts (missing sound), or distortion.

Aspect ratio: The ratio of width to height of a video frame. Common ratios are 4:3 and 16:9.

ASP: Active Server Page.

ASX: The Microsoft Windows Media Services metafile file type.

Authentication: A process that ensures a user is authorized to access a file or service.

AVI: Audio Video Interleaved. A standard uncompressed or compressed video format for personal computers.

Back light: A light shone behind a subject to bring it out of the background.

Bandwidth: The amount of data that can be transmitted over a network in a given moment.

Bit: A single unit of data.

Bit rate: The flow rate of data (bits) over a computer network.

Broadband: Usually refers to DSL and/or cable residential and small-business Internet connections, though it may sometimes refer to higher data rates available on bigger connections.

Browser: A software application that displays text, graphics, and some multimedia files downloaded from World Wide Web servers.

Buffer: A portion of RAM reserved for storing streaming data before rendering by a media player.

Byte: A unit of data comprised of bits.

Cable: 1. An insulated length of wiring connecting two hardware devices. 2. An Internet connection through a cable television operator.

Capturing: The process of recording or transferring audio and/or video information from a recording device, such as a camera, to a computer hard drive.

CD: Compact Disc.

CD-ROM: Compact Disc, Read-Only Memory.

Client: Hardware or software primarily used for receiving and rendering information sent by a server.

Client/Server: A network architecture in which one computer performs a number of dedicated tasks that serve the needs of several other computers or "workstations."

Codec: Short for COde/DECode or COmpress/DECcompress. Usually refers to a mathematical formula that removes data from a source audio or video file, leaving a smaller file suitable for streaming over a network. A codec is also used by media players to decompress streaming files.

Compression: 1. A signal processing technique whereby the peak volume levels are lowered (attenuated) to reduce distortion. 2. A technique that reduces the amount of storage space needed by a file.

Compressor: A hardware device or software application that compresses audio signals.

Connectivity: A connection to the Internet.

Connector: A hardware device that connects a cable to another cable or other hardware device. They are usually divided into male/female pairs. Common connectors in audio and video production include mini-plug, quarter-inch, RCA, XLR, and BNC.

CBR: Constant Bit Rate. A constant or steady rate of a fixed amount of data traversing the Internet between a server and a client.

Container tag: An HTML or SMIL tag enclosing other data, often to define its display or action.

Copyright: The right to give someone permission before he or she can copy a work.

Covering shot: A brief amount of video that covers a jump cut.

CPU: Central Processing Unit. The main processor of a computer.

Crop: Removing unwanted portions of a frame, similar to cropping in photography.

DC (Direct Current) offset: A method for removing inaudible noise introduced into audio when recording equipment isn't grounded properly.

Decompression: The process a media player uses to read a compressed file.

Deinterlacing: The process of removing video artifacts introduced when one video frame overlaps or interlaces with another.

Dialup: A method for connecting to the Internet with a modem, usually at 56 kilobytes per second.

Difference frame: Frames in a compressed video file containing image information that changes after a key frame is introduced.

Digital: Describes data divided into discrete binary units, often referred to as 1s and 0s.

Distributed Content: A model of file distribution based on peer-to-peer networking.

DMZ: Demilitarized Zone. A peripheral sub-network outside a firewall. Streaming servers are sometimes placed in a DMZ.

Domain: A group of networked computers with a common address.

DRM: Digital Rights Management. DRM technologies protect copyrighted content from unauthorized distribution.

DSL: Digital Subscriber Line. A broadband connection carrying Internet and voice traffic over the same copper telephone line.

DVD: Digital Video Disc.

Dynamic range: The range of a sound from silence to its loudest point.

Editing: The process of removing unwanted portions of an audio or video file. May include rearrangement of the remaining information.

Embedded: An application is said to be embedded if it performs its task within a browser window.

Encoder: A software application that converts source files into streaming media files. Sometimes called a "producer."

Encoding: The process of converting a source audio or video file into a smaller file designed for streaming media delivery.

Encryption: A method of scrambling data used in digital rights management (DRM).

EQ: Equalization (see below).

Equalization: A signal-processing technique that raises (boosts) or lowers (attenuates) the volume of audio within a certain frequency range.

Ethernet: The dominant method of networking computers.

Extension: Additions to the implementation of an open standard that differentiate the implementation from competitors while maintaining compatibility with the standard.

File: A file stores information. A streaming file stores compressed audio and video information.

FTP: File Transfer Protocol. The network communications protocol used by FTP client software to transfer files from one computer to another, usually for storage.

Fill light: A light used to fill shadows on a subject caused by the key light.

Filter: A hardware device or software application that removes unwanted image artifacts or sound from a file.

Firewall: Any of a number of software applications or hardware devices that limit the types of data that pass into or out of a computer network.

Flash: An animation technology common on the World Wide Web, developed by Macromedia.

Format: A way to organize data on a storage medium, such as a CD.

Frame: A single image in a video file, analogous to a single image in motion picture film.

Frame rate: The number of frames shown per second.

Frame size: The pixel dimensions of a frame. Sometimes expressed as an aspect ratio, often 4:3.

Freeware: Open source software.

GB: Gigabyte.

GPL: General Public License. The most widely used open source license.

HDTV: High-Definition Television, sometimes called "HD."

Headroom: 1. The amount of volume available before the sound distorts. 2. A portion of a stream reserved for non-audio or video network packets needed for proper stream performance.

Helper application: A piece of software that assists the browser when it cannot render a file. Most streaming media players are helper applications.

Hertz: A unit of measure for audio frequency.

Hyper-Text Markup Language (HTML): The standard language for creating pages rendered in a web browser.

Hyper-Text Transfer Protocol (HTTP): The standard communications protocol for delivering most kinds of traffic on the World Wide Web.

HTTP cloaking: A method for sending streams through firewalls.

HTTP streaming: Progressive downloading.

HREF: Hypertext REFerence. The "link" on a web page.

IDE: Integrated Drive Electronics. A type of hard drive interface.

IEC: International Electro-technical Committee.

IEEE: Institute of Electrical and Electronics Engineers.

IEEE 1394: Also referred to as "FireWire" or iLink. An engineering standard related to high-speed data transfer between electronic devices.

IETF: Internet Engineering Task Force.

iLink: See IEEE 1394.

Input: Data that flows into a hardware device or software application.

Intranet: A private computer network that functions like the Internet.

Inverse telecine: The process of removing duplicate frames from a video introduced when film content is transferred to video format.

IP: Internet Protocol. The standard networking protocol for computers connected to the Internet.

IP Address: The numeric Internet address of a computer.

ISO: International Standards Organization.

ISP: Internet Service Provider. An organization that provides connections to the Internet and other services, such as website hosting.

JPEG: Joint Picture Experts Group. 1. A graphics standards group. 2. A still image compression standard.

Jump cut: A video edit manifested as a sudden change in an image that is not a scene or shot change.

Kbps: Kilobytes per second. An expression of bit rate.

Key frame: A frame in a compressed video that contains information about the entire frame. Its counterpart, the difference frame, contains only information different from the key frame.

Key light: A light used to illuminate the front of a subject.

Khz: Kilohertz.

Knowledge base: An online archive of experience related to a piece of software.

LAN: Local Area Network.

Lavalier: A type of microphone used in video production.

LED: Light Emitting Diode. In audio and video production, LEDs are often used to display audio volume.

Letterbox: Describes the shape of an image with a 16:9 aspect ratio superimposed on frame with a 4:3 aspect ratio.

Live Encoding: Encoding an audio or video signal as it is created, usually for immediate distribution to an audience.

Log: A text file that records the activity of a server.

Lossless: Refers to codecs that store all input to a file.

Lossy: Refers to codecs that remove data before storing information to a file.

MB: Megabyte.

MBONE: Multimedia Back Bone. An early attempt at high-speed Internet transfer of audio and video information.

MBR: Multiple Bit Rate. The combination of several bit rates into a single encoded file.

Metadata: Data that describes other data.

Metafile: A file that contains metadata.

Mic: Microphone.

MIME type: MIME (Multipurpose Internet Mail Extensions) types are expressed as file extensions, which a software client, usually a web browser, uses to decide how to render an incoming file. When a browser encounters a streaming MIME type, it usually hands off rendering to a streaming media player.

MMS: Microsoft Media Services. A proprietary streaming protocol developed by Microsoft.

Modem: The part of a computer that allows it to connect to the Internet. Modems come in several types, including dialup, DSL, and cable.

Monitor: A hardware device for hearing audio output (speaker) or viewing video output.

Mount point: The place in the server's directory structure where streaming files are located. Several sub-directories or folders may lie under the mount point. Sometimes called the "publishing point" in Microsoft products.

MOV: A standard format for storing audio and video information, often associated with Apple Computer.

MP3: MPEG Audio Layer III. An open standard audio codec approved by the Motion Picture Experts Group.

MPEG: Motion Pictures Experts Group

MPEG-4: An MPEG open standard usually associated with video compression, though it can be used for other data types, such as still images.

MPG: A file extension for the MPEG format.

Multicast: A means of streaming to a large audience. Clients connect to a stream via a specially configured router, rather than the server delivering the stream. The counterpart to multicast is unicast.

Network: Two or more computers connected together for the purpose of communication and resource sharing.

Noise: Unwanted video artifacts or sound in a file.

Noise reduction: A complex algorithm for removing unwanted sound or video artifacts.

Non-linear editing: Describes the process of moving sections of audio or video around in a software application.

Normalization: A signal-processing technique whereby an audio signal is turned up as high as possible before distortion occurs.

On-demand: Describes a stored streaming media file that is available to a user whenever the user requests it.

On-the-fly: Refers to the creation of a file at the moment the user requests it.

Open source: A software philosophy and licensing arrangement that makes the underlying code of software available to users for viewing and modification.

Open standard: An engineering standard that manufacturers agree to follow to ensure compatibility with each other's devices.

Optimize: The process of improving the quality of data in a captured audio or video file.

OS: Operating system. The software that manages the communication between a software application and computer hardware. Microsoft Windows, Linux, and Apple's OS X are operating systems.

Output: Data that flows out of a hardware device or software application.

Outsourcing: The process of contracting a third party to perform some or all services related to streaming media.

Overhead: Data in the stream that controls streaming performance.

Overscan: The area of a video image usually covered by the plastic casing of a TV monitor. Overscan is usually removed before encoding.

P2P: Peer-to-peer streaming (See Peer-to-peer below).

Packet: A discrete chunk of data with control and addressing information sent over the Internet.

Patch: Computer code that fixes a problem.

Path: The list of directories, usually separated by the forward slash character ("/"), leading from the streaming server mount point to the streaming file.

Peer-to-peer: A network architecture in which all the computers share equal status.

Pixel: The basic unit of composition of the video image on a monitor.

Player: Also media player. A software application that renders streaming media files.

Plug-in: A software application that renders audio and video data within a web browser window.

PNA: Progressive Networks Audio. An early proprietary streaming protocol developed by RealNetworks.

Port: A number in a URL that determines which application on a server handles the data request.

Proc amp: Short for processing amplifier. A software application or hardware device that adjusts the quality of a video signal.

Progressive download: A streaming media method using the HTTP protocol.

Proprietary: Refers to the practice of keeping certain methods private to create or protect a competitive advantage.

Protocol: A set of rules that govern the exchange of data over a computer network.

Proxy: A special type of server that acts as a middleman between a user and the Internet.

Pseudo-streaming: See Progressive downloading.

QTL: The Apple Computer streaming metafile file type.

RAM: 1. Random Access Memory. The part of a computer that stores data temporarily. 2. The RealNetworks Helix System metafile file type.

RTCP: Real Time Control Protocol. An open standard protocol that works with RTP packets to check the delivery of other packets.

RTP: Real Time Transport Protocol. An open standard protocol defining rules for identifying the type of streaming packet, how packets are numbered in sequence, and how they are stamped with the date and time.

RTSP: Real Time Streaming Protocol. An open standard application level protocol used by Internet clients, i.e., media players, to talk to streaming servers.

Rebuffering: Action by a media player to gather more data in its buffer before continuing playback.

Rendering: The process of saving certain changes, usually effects, to an audio or video file.

ROI: Return on Investment.

SCSI: Small Computer System Interface, pronounced "scuzzy." A method of connecting peripheral devices to a computer, usually a hard drive.

Server: Computer hardware and software that acts solely as a central storage and distribution device for computer files. In streaming, two types of servers, web servers and media servers, typically work together.

Simultaneous streams: The number of streams sent at one time by a server. Some streaming server licenses are priced according to the number of simultaneous streams allowed.

Slide: A frame containing title or other information about a video.

Slideshow: A SMIL application in which a set of images is displayed in sequence, often with an audio track.

SMPTE: Society of Motion Picture and Television Engineers.

SMIL: Synchronized Multimedia Integration Language. An open standard markup language designed specifically for combining content types that change over time. Pronounced "smile."

Sound card: Also called audio card. The part of a computer that handles audio data.

Source file: A file before it is compressed into streaming media format. Sometimes called a "raw" file.

Standard: A set of engineering principles often based on patented ideas.

Storage: The permanent or semi-permanent repository of a file on a hard drive, CD, or DVD.

Storyboard: A series of pre-production drawings that describe the shots in a video sequence.

Streamie: A frequent user of streaming media.

Streaming media: The process of sending a time-based computer file, such as audio or video, with a streaming media server over the Internet to be rendered in real time by a streaming media client.

Tag: Code in HTML or SMIL that defines data or assigns parameters to data.

TCP: Transmission Control Protocol. One of the basic Internet communication protocols.

UDP: User Datagram Protocol. A common Internet protocol used for sending data in a continuous stream.

Uncompressed: Refers to a file in which none of the input data is removed before storage.

Unicast: A streaming media method whereby each client is sent a copy of a file. The counterpart is multicast.

URL: Uniform Resource Locater. The standard method of addressing a file on a computer connected to the Internet.

VBR: Variable Bit Rate. A method of encoding a file related to hardware device data transfers.

Video card: Hardware in a computer that handles video data displayed on a computer monitor.

Video capture card: Hardware in a computer that takes in video data from an outside source and stores it on a hard drive or other storage device.

VTR: Video Tape Recorder.

VU: Volume Unit. An expression of audio volume or loudness.

WAV: A standard method for storing audio information. Pronounced "wave."

Webcast: A live broadcast on the web.

XML: eXtensible Markup Language.

XML compliant: Conforms to XML syntax (See XML above).

YUY2: A 4:2:2 pixel format.

Index